HIDDEN HISTORY
of
LOUISIANA'S JAZZ AGE

HIDDEN HISTORY
of
LOUISIANA'S JAZZ AGE

SAM IRWIN

Foreword by Ricky Riccardi

THE
History
PRESS

Published by The History Press
Charleston, SC
www.historypress.com

Copyright © 2023 by Sam Irwin
All rights reserved

First published 2023

Manufactured in the United States

ISBN 9781467153423

Library of Congress Control Number: 2022944973

Allen Toussaint was a blessed man. Because I was born and raised in Louisiana, Toussaint was always near, but I never fully appreciated him until he was gone. That's the day I heard his album The Bright Mississippi. *Toussaint, Nicholas Payton, Don Byron, Marc Ribot, David Piltch, Jay Bellerose, Brad Mehldau and Joshua Redman, you guys made me pick up my horn and blow.*

Special shout-out to Nicholas Payton—you make it sound so easy. Thanks for reintroducing me to my trumpet.

And to my mother, Mary Grace Amy Irwin. Thanks for buying me a trumpet.

CONTENTS

FOREWORD

In writing the foreword to Sam Irwin's *Hidden History of Louisiana's Jazz Age*, I must be forthright with my own connection to the "hidden history" of Louisiana music. In 1995, while a fifteen-year-old kid living on the Jersey Shore, I was bitten by not one, not two, but three legendary New Orleans–related acts: Louis Prima, the Preservation Hall Jazz Band and, eventually, Louis Armstrong. Discovering the latter turned my life upside down for good, and nothing has ever been the same since. As I immersed myself deeper and deeper into the history, culture and especially the music of New Orleans, my mother casually remarked, "You know, Uncle Joe used to go visit our cousins in New Orleans all the time."

Uncle Joe Giardina—my mother's maiden name—was my grandfather's brother and a fixture at holiday gatherings for the first twenty or so years of my life. It was cool that we had cousins in New Orleans, but I never asked further about it, assuming they were just some benign relatives who probably took my aunt and uncle out for oysters when in town and not much else. It wasn't until a few years after my uncle passed away that I was thumbing through Al Rose's *New Orleans Jazz: A Family Scrapbook* and was stopped dead in my tracks with entries for Ernest Giardina (born in 1870 and a "leader of an early ragtime band") and Tony Giardina (a "jazz pioneer" who played with the Reliance Brass Band, Brunies brothers and members of the Original Dixieland Jazz Band). What's more, there was a photo of Tony Giardina, and he looked just like Uncle Joe, only playing a clarinet! I also discovered Tony was a barber by trade—my grandfather's profession.

By this point, you might be wondering what any of this has to do with Sam Irwin's wonderful book, but it's just a personal reflection/realization that the hidden history of Louisiana's jazz age runs *deep*, with "pioneers" of the music sometimes remaining unknown to their own descendants.

To discover and pay tribute to every single early pioneer of New Orleans music would take a full set of encyclopedias (remember those?). But Sam Irwin has done the world a service in this volume, combining exciting new research and a gripping style of storytelling that will be appreciated by the historians of the music but will also be gobbled up by the average fan who might be familiar with the names of Louis Armstrong and Buddy Bolden but assuredly has not spent much time with the danger-ridden early career of clarinetist Joe Darensbourg or the shocking demise of trumpeter Evan Thomas.

In my last paragraph, I made the error of referring solely to "New Orleans music," which can lead some to assume that every great musician who ended up settling in that fabled city was born and raised there. Irwin makes it clear to his readers that Louisiana is a big state, and some of its most important musicians and bands actually emanated from rural areas and other major cities, not just the Crescent one. Was I aware of the importance of "unsung hero" Toots Johnson on the Baton Rouge music scene? I was not but am glad I am now.

Baton Rouge is also the setting of one of the book's multiple chapters on Louis Armstrong, perhaps the most written-about figure in the entire history of jazz (I know of what I speak, as I'm currently in the midst of writing my third full-length biography of the trumpeter). Even with a wealth of published material on the subject already easily available, Irwin finds new, unexplored ways of presenting Satchmo, not just writing about his aforementioned early Baton Rouge experiences but also detailing Armstrong's eventful returns home in 1931 and 1945. Irwin even provides a new spin on the old controversy about Armstrong's birthday that is mandatory reading for all fans of New Orleans's most famous son.

I can go on detailing and previewing the events that are to take place in the ensuing pages, but I don't want to spoil the fun. Some jazz histories get lost in music theory, bogged down in discussions of the notes and rhythms the musicians played, as important as those attributes are. Irwin, a fine trumpet man himself, knows that it's the off-the-bandstand events—issues of race, jealousy, even murder—that fueled the formation of this music, and by treating those situations and the musicians involved with the respect they deserve, he has made a lasting contribution to jazz scholarship.

The history of Louisiana's Jazz Age might be a little less hidden now, thanks to Sam Irwin's work, and one can only hope others follow his lead to continue to explore other unsung heroes and untold tales from the state that has provided the most lasting soundtrack to the American experience in all of its forms, good, bad, ugly—and swinging.

—Ricky Riccardi
August 2022

Ricky Riccardi is the director of Research Collections for the Louis Armstrong House Museum and author of two biographies of Armstrong, What a Wonderful World *and* Heart Full of Rhythm. *He won a Grammy in 2022 in the Best Album Notes category and has presented Armstrong lectures around the world.*

PREFACE

When Nicholas Payton's performance on "Egyptian Fantasy" from Allen Toussaint's *The Bright Mississippi* album inspired me to pick up my trumpet after a thirty-year layoff, I rediscovered the jazz of Louisiana. I say rediscovered because when you grow up in south Louisiana, great music is all around you.

As a kid from Breaux Bridge, I was aware of Louis Armstrong's fame and proud that he was from New Orleans. I heard Al Hirt's "Java" accompany the Muppets on *Ed Sullivan*. I knew Pete Fountain played clarinet. We drove down Bourbon Street (remember when you could do that?), and I saw their clubs from the back seat of my parents' car. And somehow, even in Breaux Bridge, everyone knew "When the Saints Go Marching In" was a revered state song.

I was more familiar with French music and swamp pop. I had the good fortune to grow up two blocks away from La Poussiere, my hometown's famous Cajun music club. On those splendid Sunday southern nights, I could easily hear the steady bass *chanky-chank* beat from Larry Brasseaux's band from my bedroom window, and I can't tell you how many times I heard the swamp pop sounds of Rod Bernard's "Colinda" emanate from the jukebox at Robin's Club, which was across the gravel road from my grandparents' home in Henderson.

My grandmother loved music and had plenty of Fats Domino's 45s to go along with her Aldus Rogér records. Cajun and New Orleans rhythm and blues beats were everywhere. Once, when I was a child walking across the

Bayou Teche drawbridge, I crossed paths with a young Black man headed in the opposite direction. He was singing, "Baby, my time is too expensive… and I'm not a little boy." Everyone in south Louisiana knows the lyrics to Aaron Neville's "Tell It Like It Is" and can sing it at the drop of a hat; it's practically a state requirement.

For someone musically inclined, south Louisiana is a gold mine, but it wasn't until Allen Toussaint assembled and recorded an amazing lineup of traditional jazz tunes on *The Bright Mississippi* that I became aware of the role Louisiana musicians played in creating jazz and all the other forms of pop music that evolved from it.

I grew up with the Beatles and played my share in rock bands in the 1970s and '80s. For every John, Paul, George and Ringo, there were thousands of Larrys, Bobbys, Tims, Charleys, Lisas, Sallys and Marys who played that old-time rock-and-roll and never made it past their parish line. Likewise, for every great jazz musician who came out of New Orleans and made it "big," there were dozens of musicians who played gigs in smoky bars, the dumps, the lawn parties and the funeral parades for a little bit of money and a lot of fun.

I found the untold stories of Louisiana's early twentieth-century jazz musicians to be quite fascinating. I tried to tell the how and why of their circumstances. Ultimately, the reader will judge if I've done a good job with their history. I've enjoyed the journey.

Acknowledgements

I never set out to be a writer, but now I've made my living at it for almost twenty years. It's very clear to me that I could have never become a writer without the encouragement and support of my wife, Betty Dupont of Plaquemine, a Mississippi River town. She never tires (if she does, she disguises it well) of hearing me say, "Listen to what I learned today!"

My pal Emily Cogburn, who somehow ended up in Louisiana after growing up in Minnesota, has always been my go-to reader and editor. She is a persistent novelist, and it's only a matter of time before she hits it big.

Wallace McKenzie, whom I sang with for years in the Baton Rouge Symphony Chorus (and never knew he was a music history professor), and his PhD student Charles Kinzer played a role in the writing of this book. Dr. Kinzer unwittingly became a big inspiration to me as I stumbled on his amazing biography of the musical Tio family of New Orleans. Did Jim Dormon—a retired history professor from my alma mater, the University of Louisiana at Lafayette, and the first to read my supposition about Louis Armstrong's birthday—give me enough encouraging words to write a book? No, but at least another blog post. And guess what? After a few more posts, there was enough for a book. Sure do miss you, Jim. My old pal from UL graduate school days, Dr. Chris Nordmann, helped me out with the genealogy questions, as did professional genealogist Judy Riffel of Baton Rouge. Author Steve Luxenberg and poet Patrice Melnick offered sage advice.

Ricky Riccardi of the Louis Armstrong Museum provided gold nuggets of Louis Armstrong wisdom, as did historic geographer Richard Campanella of

New Orleans. Ricky won a Grammy award for his liner notes on *The Complete Louis Armstrong Columbia and RCA Victor Studio Sessions 1946–1966,* and he should win an award for the foreword he wrote for this book. Louisiana roots music writer and researcher Gene Tomko has an encyclopedic knowledge of Bayou State's musicians. Author-folklorist-musician Ben Sandmel, thank you for your editorial expertise. Amanda Fallis at the New Orleans Public Library is such a great librarian and very professional. Philip Cunningham of Tulane Research Services now knows the *Louisiana Weekly* newspaper archive very well and was a big help. Jazz historian John McCusker provided some salient points. Jan Ramsey of *Offbeat* magazine, thanks for publishing that great journal. The New Orleans Jazz Museum (thank you, Christina Stebbins), Hogan Jazz Archive at Tulane University and Rutgers University Institute of Jazz Studies are wonderful resources, and I thank you for your assistance. The East Baton Rouge Parish Library has a wonderful digital archive, and I couldn't have written this book without its great collections of Baton Rouge and New Orleans newspapers.

I have come to know and love a cadre of "older" folks who have inspired me to play, perform and write: John Dupaquier, ninety-two, is an emeritus member of the Florida Street Blowhards. He's forgotten more jazz than I'll ever know. Even if he doesn't know the song, he knows it. The same for Dr. Joe Lamendola, ninety, the leader of the Rampart Street Six. He talks just the way you would expect a jazz trumpeter to talk. Retired LSU English professor (and pioneering Sun Records A&R rep) Barbara Sims, eighty-eight, author of *The Next Elvis*, has been a loyal member of the Florida Street Blowhards' audience.

But most of all, many thanks go to the musicians of New Orleans and its hinterlands who created jazz. They endured. They practiced. They performed. They were great.

INTRODUCTION

There is no place like Louisiana. In addition to jazz, Louisiana created Cajun music, the cowboy,[1] zydeco and crawfish. It perfected the *fais do do* (street dance), the *bal de maison*, culinary artistry, bad politics and *joie de vivre*.

Where else could a Frenchman born in Montreal and destined to become a Louisiana colonial governor celebrate Mardi Gras in the swamp in 1699? New Orleans, of course. Who does that? *Les bons vivants de la Louisiane*, that's who.

Where else will a solemn brass band in a "jazz funeral" escort you to your aboveground tomb and then transform into a joyous jazz band to lead your family and friends in revelry for your presumed entrance into heaven?

And where else could the lead marker emblazoned with the seal of France on it left by LaSalle in 1671 at the mouth of the Mississippi River be found by a twentieth-century fisherman who cut it into small pieces, which he used to weigh down his shrimp nets?[2]

Despite this lack ("it ain't dere no more" syndrome)[3] of preservation (we tore down Storyville, Charity Hospital and Louis Armstrong's birthplace; fenced off Congo Square; and let Buddy Bolden's house slip into disrepair), Louisiana, and specifically New Orleans, created jazz, and it came from an incredible series of events that could not have happened anywhere else in the world. Why? Because its unique Creole society was "West Indian in origin, French in speech, Catholic in belief, European in its dominant taste."[4] (Disclaimer: there is no consensus on what the word *Creole* means.

Buddy Bolden's house at 2309–11 First Street in New Orleans's Central City neighborhood. Jazz historian John McCusker says, "If New Orleans is known as the cradle of jazz, then the Bolden house is the crib." This was the house Bolden was living in when he had his mental breakdown in 1906. *Sam Irwin photo.*

Any mention of Creole in this book is subjective and does not endorse or dismiss any other interpretation of the word. See Ben Sandmel's *Zydeco* for a discussion of the term.)

Wynton Marsalis, perhaps jazz's most visible spokesperson, believes, "Every strand of American music comes directly from Congo Square."[5] He calls jazz the "mulatto identity of our national music,"[6] which simmered in a nineteenth-century gumbo seasoned with a dash of voodoo; a serving of *le danse*; generous helpings of *l'opera*, musicianship, European military parades, religious processions, sanctified churches, the Great Migration and street vending; and serious dollops of Mardi Gras, decadence and geography.

If one were to promenade around the 1803 French Quarter, one might have heard a hummed operatic aria on Bourbon Street, an African chant on the wharfs along Levee (now Decatur) Street, West Indian ditties in the back o' town, martial airs performed by crude brass bands in the Place D'Armes (Jackson Square) and a brass band trudging to a funeral dirge in St. Louis Cemetery. New Orleans in the nineteenth century was a "peculiarly open public domain—the street as theatre—a field of anarchy steeped in the cultural residue of Mediterranean Europe."[7] All of these cultural influences were wonderfully common in New Orleans and foreign anywhere else in English-speaking America.

Jazz had been percolating in a "core [of] a tight-knit Creole establishment of classical orientation, descended from the *ancienne* population; at least two dozen performers of Caribbean and Mexican origin, and a small but influential contingent of Sicilians....Many immigrant Sicilians had played brass in the island's peasant army bands."[8]

The Creoles of color, of French and Spanish heritage, made up a third tier of social class in New Orleans, but their status was slowly eroded by the American racial attitudes and laws of the time, culminating in the passage of an 1894 state law that defined all persons with any African ancestry as "Negros"[9] and the infamous *Plessy v. Ferguson* Supreme Court ruling of 1896, "which drove Creoles and blacks together in a common alienation."[10] This "common alienation" collaborated with the musical innovation of Buddy Bolden, an Americanized Black man, and defined jazz.

We don't have a recording of Buddy Bolden (a cylinder may have been recorded, but it was lost),[11] but whatever twist he put on the music of New Orleans set the establishment on its ear (pun intended). The "old heads" like Lorenzo "Papa" Tio instructed students to play with a pretty tone and precision; Bolden explored timbre and learned a style, "a way of hesitating" to get behind and catch up to the beat. In 1900, he might not have been the first trumpet player to do so, but it has been agreed that "he was the first great cornet player to do it."[12]

The year 1900 was the beginning of a new century. The Black public ear demanded something new, and they chose Bolden. The refined white audience still preferred the sweet music of the lighter-skinned Creoles, but Bolden played the music the Black community liked, and if the Creoles wanted to get regular paying gigs, they had to play like Bolden. Establishment New Orleans resisted the sum total of all this outrageous fortune, but jazz became the most significant art form America has ever produced.

Chapter 1

MURDER ON THE BANDSTAND

When New Orleans native Sam Theard wrote "I'll Be Glad When You're Dead, You Rascal, You," he was most likely doing what every songwriter tries to do: write a hit song. A Black American songwriter, actor, entertainer and comedian, Theard tried on for size several different personas through the years. He was known on the chitlin circuit as Lovin' Sam from Down in 'Bam, where he developed his art of the "hokum" lyric and recorded a rocking tune called "Spo-De-Odee," one of the many slang terms he coined that meant sexual intercourse. "Adam met Eve in the Garden of Eden, that's where it first begun; Adam said to Eve, 'Let's spo-dee-o-dee, come on, let's have some fun,'" he sang in his minor hit.[13] Later, he recorded as Spo-De-Odee.

He had a recurring role in the last season of *Sanford and Son* and a small part in Richard Pryor's *Which Way Is Up*. His unique look and gravelly voice landed him spots in *Little House on the Prairie* and *The Sting II*. His enduring contribution to pop culture was for his role in writing and/or contributing to three notable songs: "Rock Around the Clock" (a hit for Bill Haley), "Let the Good Times Roll" (a 1942 hit for Louis Jordan; also known to south Louisiana zydeco audiences as "Laissez Les Bon Temps Rouler") and "I'll Be Glad When You're Dead, You Rascal, You."

Written when Theard was twenty-five years old, "IBGWYDYRY" became a hit for several of the best-known musical acts in the 1930s and beyond. Among the varied hitmakers are the Mills Brothers, an African American jazz and blues singing quartet most popular in the 1930s; New

Orleans–born early jazz soprano saxophonist innovator Sidney Bechet; 1930s pianist and prolific composer Fats Waller; saxophonist, bandleader and 1930–40s "Jukebox King"[14] Louis Jordan; New Orleans swing king Louis Prima; 1960s–70s songwriter John Fogerty; roots bluesman Taj Mahal; provocative French pop singer Serge Gainsbourg; twenty-first-century singer-songwriter Hanni El Khatib; and pianist-songwriter and New Orleans culture maven Dr. John.[15]

Born in 1904, Theard grew up in segregated New Orleans, where Black people always had to "give whites the wall" or else.[16] Since Louis Armstrong was born in 1901, it's very likely their paths crossed. There were limited opportunities in the Crescent City for young Black men like Louis and Sam: you could be a laborer, or you could be a musician. There were plenty of opportunities to entertain in Storyville. Theard, like Louis, chose the raucous, roustabout lifestyle of a performer. Since he was clever and decided to live by his wits, he joined the tent circuit and the circus after finishing whatever schooling he got in Louisiana.

Black people in the Jim Crow era in the North and South had to go along to get along, and Sam quickly learned what his professional role was: to write bawdy songs "loaded with double-entendres and gritty details about African American life."[17]

Theard wrote and recorded "I'll Be Glad When You're Dead, You Rascal, You" in 1929. Tampa Red and Fats Waller's version quickly followed and helped popularize the song with Black audiences.[18] On the surface, the song is loaded with Pagliacci-like "laugh at my pain" lyrics, but even with the amusing rhymes, the tune didn't go very far for Theard, at least on the charts. But for Black artists and audiences, the song—like the slave songs of the past that veiled their yearning for freedom under the pretense of a religious context— would provide an obvious hidden transcript for Black performers that would last for decades. It could be interpreted as a message to society to kill prejudice and racism.[19] With Theard's reputation for penning funny songs about Black life, the message must have gone over the heads of the white audience.

Curiously, it was a white musician, cornetist Red Nichols, who introduced the song to the mainstream audience. He made the song a bit more palatable to the masses by taking out Theard's threat of castration to his rival ("I'm gonna cut your arms off too, and something else that's attached to you"), which seemed to open the door for Black performers. According to *Joel Whitburn's Pop Memories*, Nichols's version went to #14. Cab Calloway brought it to #17. Armstrong hit it up to #13. The following year, the Mills Brothers' version reached #3.[20]

But Satchmo's versions brought the most popularity to the Rascal song, and it became "indelibly associated with Armstrong…performed countless times until his passing in 1971."[21] Louis conducted, performed and appeared in *I'll Be Glad When You're Dead, You Rascal You*, a 1932 cartoon starring Betty Boop, the irrepressible Jazz Age flapper.[22] He was also featured performing the tune dressed in jungle attire in *A Rhapsody in Black and Blue*.[23]

What a perfect vehicle for Pops (Louis called everyone "Pops," and soon everyone began to refer to him as the same)[24] to convey his hidden transcript. Because he was the best trumpet player in America and because he, on the surface, knew a big part of his appeal to the white producers and audiences was the "laughing minstrel character,"[25] Louis cast a few well-placed barbs here and there at white folks. On one such occasion, pianist Errol Garner stopped by Pops's dressing room after a show and asked, "What's new?" Satchmo, without missing a beat, replied, "Nothin' new—white folks still ahead."[26]

Another time, Armstrong made his 1931 return to New Orleans and was bragging that his baseball team, the Secret Nine (a pickup team he outfitted with new uniforms),[27] was going to defeat the professional New Orleans Black Pelicans of the Negro Southern League. While on stage (and in range of the live WSMB broadcast mic, radio announcer Charles Nelson included), Louis was overheard teasing that the Secret Nine were going to "take them like Grant took Richmond."[28]

To be sure, Louis knew what was going on in the great white North and the Jim Crow South. He revealed to *Ebony* writer Charles L. Sanders in a 1964 interview:

> *Look, Pops, I come out of part of the South where it ain't no way in the world you can forget you're colored. My own mother went through hell down there. My Grandma used to have tears in her eyes when she'd talk about the lynchings and all that crap. Even myself, I've seen things that would make my flesh crawl. But it wasn't a damn thing I could do about it…and keep on breathing.*[29]

Several of the damn things he couldn't do a thing about occurred when Pops made his celebrated return to New Orleans in 1931, nine years after he left the city to claim fame and fortune, first with King Oliver's Chicago band and then as a solo artist.

Pops was in a bit of a quandary in 1931, as New York gangsters were trying to gain control of his career and the union wanted him to answer

Louis Armstrong equipped his "Secret Nine" baseball team on his first visit back to New Orleans in 1931 after being gone for nine years. He played a three-month gig at the Suburban Gardens club, where the performances were broadcast over WSMB radio. Armstrong inadvertently let slip a boast, which was picked up by the live microphone, that his Secret Nine baseball team was going to beat the professional New Orleans Pelicans "like Grant took Richmond." The remark did not go over well with the white announcer, who refused to introduce Armstrong. Armstrong introduced himself and later laughingly claimed the Nine would have won if they had been willing to slide, but the uniforms were too nice to get dirty. *Courtesy of the Louis Armstrong House Museum.*

some questions about a New York contract dispute. Louis and his band were playing one-night stands and were tired of the constant travel, and his manager at the time, Johnny Collins, booked him for three months beginning in mid-June at the Suburban Gardens in New Orleans.

Louis was worried. "I did not know whether they had forgotten about me in all the time I'd been away, because I was just 'Little Louie' Armstrong when I left and not too much account. But I soon found they had not," he wrote in his 1936 *Swing That Music* autobiography.[30] When the train pulled in at the Louisville and Nashville Station, there were four hot bands[31] at the station, the *Times-Picayune* reported (Louis remembered eight), and they were all "swinging" on the platform.[32] The *Picayune* noted there were "several thousand negroes" there to greet him but did not mention any white fans.

"They picked me up and put me on their shoulders and started a parade down the center of Canal Street," Louis said. "Those eight bands almost bust the town open they made so much noise. I think that day was the happiest day in my life."[33]

Pops saw many faces from his past, including Captain Joseph Jones and Peter Davis, his mentors from the Colored Waifs Home, that day.[34] Davis also mentored Dave Bartholomew, who went on to fame with 1950s rocker Fats Domino.[35] Jones and Davis wished Armstrong well.

White New Orleans, for the most part, was thrilled. At the Suburban Gardens, "crowds are gay" and presented "Louis Armstrong and his Recording Orchestra in an original type of rhythm that has been a national sensation where the music of Armstrong's has tempted restless feet. Suburban Gardens, always first with the best, now present a name orchestra."[36]

But this was 1931 New Orleans, and Jim Crow was never far away. It started on the first night's performance at the club. Radio broadcast was still new, and the Suburban Gardens had its own radio broadcast on WSMB. The Gardens manager, Earl Dalton, instructed radio emcee Charles Nelson, "This is a big deal now, you bring on Louis Armstrong, he's a New Orleans boy."[37]

But Nelson (and the radio audience) may have overheard Armstrong's crack on a live microphone about Grant taking Richmond, said Zilner Randolph, Armstrong's musical director.[38]

"Brother, did the letters pour in," Randolph recollected in a 1977 interview.

Nelson refused to introduce Armstrong. "This is a situation that I have never had to fight in my life before. I just can't introduce that n----r," Nelson told Dalton and Armstrong manager Johnny Collins.[39]

If Louis was offended, he didn't show it. He took it in stride.

"You never heard of no spade playing on no radio in those days," he said. "I had been away about nine years, and I done got 'northern-fied' and forgot about a whole lot of that foolishness down there."

Ever the consummate professional, Louis took the mic and hosted the show.

"It was the first time a Negro spoke on the radio down there," Armstrong said in an *Ebony* magazine interview. "And it worked out just fine."

Louis said Nelson was fired. The *Picayune* wrote of the firing with a delicate touch. "Charles Nelson, whose voice has been heard through WDSU and WSMB within the past two years, has again quit the local radio fold, though thus far he has been unable to tear himself away from the New Orleans cooking."[40]

There were other racist mishaps, but the one that brought Louis to tears was his inability to give a performance for Black New Orleans. Louis, who freely gave $500 to $1,000 away a week to folks who needed it,[41] had agreed to give a free concert for Black people at the Army Supply Base on Dauphine and Poland Streets. Thousands of his fans poured in from the small towns and the city to see their local hero play the trumpet, but on the day of the big event when the band arrived, they were confronted with a locked gate. The American Negro Press wire story, probably written by E. Belfield Spriggs of the *Louisiana Weekly*,[42] suggested the dance promoters sent the word out that rules prohibited renting the warehouse, but that didn't quiet the crowd.[43] The Black-owned *Pittsburgh Courier* reported that Armstrong tried to bring the show to the Pythian Hall, but "they found [Armand] Piron and his orchestra and Piron wouldn't give place."[44] The *Picayune* failed to pick up the story. The *Louisiana Weekly*'s Black editors did some investigation, but no explanation was delivered.

> We are forced to say that up to date, only such information has been available as is now in the possession of one of the promoters, Mr. L. Norris, who this week showed all of the permits issued to him by the city and the Douglas Warehouse Company. We have tried every way possible to locate the reasons that led to the postponement of the dance, but as yet we have met with no success.[45]

According to *Horn of Plenty*, Robert Goffin's flowery biography of Armstrong, the National Guard was called in and drove away the bitterly disappointed crowd at bayonet point.[46]

Zilner Randolph alluded to union and racial issues and attributed the lockout to a number of factors beyond Louis's control.

> The big dance—the union there, the union and the officials, the political officials got together and they wouldn't let us have it. They wouldn't let them have the dance. And the people were just like that. I don't know why they said they wouldn't let us have it, but that's just what happened. I guess, near everybody in New Orleans was getting ready to go to that—were ready for that dance. You really was right. They certainly didn't. Didn't let us have it. We really would have made the money that time. Really would have made money.[47]

The angry crowd dispersed and cursed Louis Armstrong. They didn't know Louis did everything he could to make things right, but their hero was powerless. Louis cried when they drove away from the army base, and he insisted on going to Back o' Town, his Jane Alley birthplace. There, whatever fond remembrance he had of his old neighborhood was shattered, his rose-colored glasses permanently broken. He saw Jane Alley for what it was: a trash-ridden slum where the poorest of the poor lived. He found his grandmother's house and gave her some cash; it was likely the last time he saw her. Defeated and alone, he boarded a streetcar since no taxis would travel in such a locale. He had to ride back to the hotel in the "colored only" section.[48]

If the day he arrived in New Orleans was the happiest day of his life, this may have been the saddest.

The band left New Orleans and headed west, where they played for twelve thousand fans in Houston. They hit Dallas, Tulsa, Oklahoma City and back to Dallas before heading to Memphis, Tennessee, where he experienced another tussle with the South.

The band had booked a bus with reclining seats in Memphis, but the white driver was taken aback at seeing a busload of urbanized Black men and one white woman sitting next to Louis.

"I didn't know it was going to be like this," the driver said.[49] It obviously offended the driver's white sensibilities that Louis was sitting next to the white Mrs. Collins, who had been traveling with the band throughout the South, helping to make hotel accommodations and such. The driver also eyed the musicians sporting Harlem Renaissance fashions like "fancy plus fours, bright-hued golf socks and…vari-colored berets worn in the latest Jimmy Walker style."[50] One of the musicians was even smoking a cigarette with a long fancy cigarette holder.

"The driver kept looking at my trumpet man, Zilner Randolph, who had some kind of French beret on. He began to make it clear he wasn't standing for any of this shit," Armstrong said.[51]

In other words, the driver was upset because the band looked cool and he was, well, a bus driver.

A call was made to Johnny Collins to come and sort things out, but the Memphis blues showed first, and after one cop suggested shooting Louis in the leg,[52] more police arrived.

The cops ordered everyone off the bus with the announcement, "All right, you n-----s get out of there. You're in Memphis now, and we need some cotton pickers too."[53]

The police confiscated six guns[54] but found no evidence of an enterprising band member's pimping business.[55] Instead, they hauled them off to jail, where one of the officers jeered, "You ain't gonna come down to Memphis and try to run the city. We'll kill all you n-----s."[56]

Locked in a cell with his valet, Professor Sherman Cook, Louis was always worried he'd get busted in the chops and his trumpet career would be over. Possibly the big marijuana joint the Professor had wrapped in his pocket took some of the edge off the nerve-racking day. Louis said, "Hey, man. We can't get in any more trouble than we are in right now. So, we lit up and smoked our way out of trouble. The other cats in their cells caught the smell of the stuff and they all started shouting out about passing it around but ol' Cook and myself we demolished the evidence."[57]

Collins eventually showed up with the Palace Theater promoter, who bailed them out with the promise they'd perform on a radio broadcast the next day. The Palace gig went off without incident, and the following morning, Louis made their live broadcast as promised. Cops were milling around everywhere in the studio ready to pounce if the band broke a Jim Crow code.

At this point, Louis may figuratively have said "fuck you" to the police and they didn't even know it. He leaned into the microphone and said, "Ladies and gentlemen, I am now going to dedicate this song to the Memphis police force."[58] The band hit the downbeat hard and swung into a rollicking version of Sam Theard's new hit, "I'll Be Glad When You're Dead, You Rascal, You."

What happened? Given the threats, the band was fearful. Trombonist Preston Jackson, whose family had left New Orleans in 1917 to escape police brutality, was scared.

"Some of the policemen was there, that I'd seen the day before," Jackson related. "Now whether Louis meant well by it or meant it as a slur, I don't know. We did play the song and after the broadcast they all made a dash towards us, 'bout ten or twelve of them. There was nowhere for us to run, or we would have ran, you know. But they told us, 'You're the first band that ever dedicated a tune to the Memphis Police.'"[59]

Louis Armstrong might have been the only musician who ever lived who could deliver such an obvious message to the Memphis police with no repercussion, but the hidden transcript was clear: I really will be glad when white supremacy is dead and gone.

To be fair, the *Memphis Commercial Appeal*, possibly to appear sophisticated and not embarrass the town, downplayed the entire arrest episode in two separate news stories. In "DarkTown Stage Troupe to Face Judge Instead of Arkansas Audience," the paper didn't mention Armstrong until the last paragraph and referred to his band as the "Chicago Orchestra with its New York manageress and the Dallas dancer."[60] "The negroes exhibited some pistols, six to be exact," also made it into the story, buried on page nine. In a follow-up court report, the newspaper reported the dismissed charges. The band wasn't in the headline, and again, Louis was not mentioned until the last line.[61] Even so, the band was happy to see Memphis in the rearview mirror as they hightailed it out of town.

What possessed Louis to undertake such risky behavior? Obviously, the song was the perfect retort for the nasty behavior the boorish white cops displayed toward the musicians. "I'll Be Glad When You're Dead, You Rascal, You" continued to be a hit for Pops wherever he played it. As Louis Armstrong biographer Ricky Riccardi noted, the song was daring with a subtle reference to marijuana:

The song was perfected by Armstrong at Sebastian's Cotton Club in Culver City, with multiple newspapers reporting on Armstrong's live performances (which made the radio censors quite nervous). He really sounds like he's having the time of his life here, repeating "Oh you dog" enough times that it became known as his catchphrase. There's also a line about "standing on the corner high," which is particularly daring considering Armstrong spent a few days in jail barely a month earlier because of his arrest for marijuana possession.

And how about that band! This particular outfit has always been a favorite punching bag for many critics, but they sure do swing here, especially when Tubby Hall starts cooking on those cymbals. Louis is on fire, too, vocally and with the horn.

We don't have sales numbers, but we can be assured that this record was quite a hit for him. Less than a year later, he would be filmed doing "You Rascal You" in two different Paramount shorts and even starred in a Soundie of the same name in 1942....But I love these performances, too, as they cap off the April 1931 sides with a bang.[62]

The novelty song was Sam Theard's specialty, and despite the hidden transcript, it was not to be taken seriously; after all, the cuckolded husband portrayed in "Rascal" has been a comic figure in literature for centuries.[63] But one night on a bandstand deep in the heart of Louisiana, a disgruntled ex-convict took the song at face value in the tiny town of Rayne, where a jazz band led by Evan Thomas and featuring Bunk Johnson and George Lewis was performing.

What was jazz like in southwest Louisiana? Pretty good, said clarinetist Joe Darensbourg. And Evan Thomas was the best trumpet player in those parts.

"Every little town in Louisiana had some kind of band," said Joe. "There was a good band in Alexandria led by a left-hand[ed] violin player named John Tonkin. There was another band in Lafayette and the Martel Band out of Opelousas. I worked with them, too. And they had the Black Eagles out of Crowley, that was one of the best. The Banner Band out of New Iberia had a left-hand[ed] trumpet player named Victor Spencer who was very good."[64]

Left-handed musicians notwithstanding, Darensbourg saved his highest praise for Thomas, whose band was the Black Eagles out of Crowley in Acadia Parish. Thomas also gigged with the Banner Band.

"The Banner Band out of New Iberia had Evan Thomas, a trumpet player," Darensbourg said. "He was out of this world, great! He made a trumpet sound like a violin."[65]

Darensbourg knew how a good trumpet player sounded; he was Louis Armstrong's reed man with the All Stars from 1961 to 1963 and played on Pops's 1963 recording of "Hello, Dolly."[66]

He also knew drinking; he mentions several times in *Jazz Odyssey* that he drank a lot in his younger days and sometimes mentions the drinking habits of the musicians he met on his travels. The Banner Band were big drinkers, and Evan Thomas? Well, "he drank like a fish."[67] Drinking played a sad role in Thomas's life.

In the days before television and radio, there were plenty of honky-tonks, clubs, dance halls, joints, fairs and churches for musicians to perform in. And Louisiana's bayou country, with its sugar cane and Creole cattle culture, had created a sizable enslaved population just as the Mississippi River plantation system did. Like in New Orleans, music offered poor, small-town Black residents a sliver of upward mobility in the segregated state.

According to Austin Sonnier Jr. in his slim volume *Second Linin': Jazzmen of Southwest Louisiana, 1900–1950,*[68] the style was

> *another form of music…a unique type of rural jazz. This genre, a combination of traditional New Orleans jazz, ragtime, African rhythms, Creole folk material, and the blues was from the beginning of* [the twentieth] *century a most desirable vehicle for many types of entertainment in southwest Louisiana. The jazz music of New Orleans filtered through*

to that part of the state during the early part of [the twentieth] *century and immediately influenced local musicians to try their hand at its beauty and charm. This resulted in the birth of a brother to the original New Orleans sound.*

For every jazz great who gained fame in New Orleans, there were a dozen unsung greats from the small towns of Louisiana's French and Creole parishes. Places with large Black populations like Parks, Crowley, Cade, Loreauville, Opelousas and New Iberia were mini hotbeds of jazz.[69] The musicians took lessons from professors like Joseph Oger of Crowley, who had studied at the Mozart Conservatory of Music in Paris. Professor Claiborne Williams was the professional in Donaldsonville, and the Howe Institute of New Iberia, a school for Black people, taught music as well. Some of the small-town musicians spent time in New Orleans and studied with Lorenzo Tio Jr. Others, like Bunk Johnson and Lawrence Duhé, started in New Orleans and ended up in Acadiana.[70] Rural jazz was performed by the Hypolite Charles Band, Yelpin' Hounds, Banner Band, Adam Jenkins Band, United Brass Band, Black Diamond Band, Victory Band, Night Hawks and the Black Eagle Band.[71]

For every big name in early jazz, like Louis Armstrong, Jelly Roll Morton and Sidney Bechet, who were New Orleans natives, there were plenty of other big names who originated in small towns. Kid Ory was from LaPlace, Zutty Singleton was born in Bunkie, Joe "King" Oliver came from Aben and Pops Foster hailed from McCall, just a mile or two from Aben.[72] These musicians and their families migrated to the opportunity of New Orleans (known as *"la Ville"*[73] to Louisiana's French-speaking residents) and made a significant mark in the jazz world. But there were hundreds of small-town musicians who were largely ignored by jazz producers and historians.

Geography, it seems, played a sizable role in the absence of recording activity. New Orleans where the bulk of music traffic was centered, was too far away and record producers were content with exploiting the talent there anyway. Nobody took much interest in going off to "discover" anyone after Bunk Johnson. Surely economic and social factors also played their part. So, the best years of some of Louisiana's finest musicians just went up in sound.[74]

Rural jazzmen played the blues, and the "hot" arrangements of the popular songs of the times and "Rascal" became a fun standard to perform for country audiences. The burlesque violence of the song was laughable, but on November 21, 1931, John Guillory took the song literally and attacked Evan Thomas of the Black Eagle Band on the bandstand in Rayne.

Evan Thomas of Crowley was born on January 6, 1894, and studied under Professor Joseph Oger. Acadia Parish musicians held the Professor in high regard and believed "that old man knew just about everything about music."[75] Thomas was in demand and had a regular gig for years with Gus Fontenette's highly regarded Banner Orchestra of New Iberia. Bunk Johnson had settled in New Iberia and played second trumpet in the Banner Orchestra with Thomas, who also hired Johnson for work in his own band, the Black Eagle Band out of Crowley. Identifying his band as "Black" called attention to the band's racial identity and signified a pride in their ethnicity, suggested Louisiana roots music writer and researcher Gene Tomko.[76]

Thomas and Johnson were all about the music, and the younger Thomas peppered the more experienced Johnson with questions about music and jazz.

"Him and Bunk used to get into big arguments about music," said musician Harold Potier, a contemporary of Thomas. "Do you know where they would go to settle them? At Professor Oger's house in Crowley, that's where."[77]

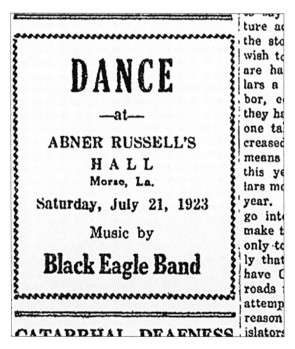

Unusual for the time, Evan Thomas appeared to celebrate his band's ethnicity by calling it the Black Eagle Band. The eagle of freedom held special significance to African Americans in the nineteenth century, and several early jazz bands (Frankie Duson's Eagle Band, Young Eagle Band, Happy Eagle Orchestra) adopted the eagle name and were very popular throughout New Orleans and Louisiana. *From the* Crowley Post-Signal, *Crowley, Louisiana.*

Bunk would have always thought he was right, the record suggests. Jazz historian Al Rose said, "Bunk Johnson could be very unpleasant, especially to other musicians, few of whom he respected."[78]

Bunk's playing in the 1920s was that of a "sweet trumpet player," said Potier. "From below the staff and in the staff, he was one of the sweetest trumpet players I ever heard. He had melody down pat…real lyrical."[79]

Evan, on the other hand, was "more of a blues king," said reed man Morris Dauphine, also of Parks. "He could play you a blues like nobody else."[80]

Dauphine studied at the Howe Institute in New Iberia, a private academy for Black people built in 1887.[81] In 1925, he moved to New Orleans and took lessons from Lorenzo Tio Jr. and played with Oscar "Papa" Celestin's Tuxedo Band for two years.[82]

Thomas's playing was on par with the top trumpet players of the day, said clarinetist Lawrence Duhé.

"I've never heard no one no better than E.T. Thomas," Duhé told jazz researcher William Russell. "For high work, high register, he was as good as Louis Armstrong in those days."[83]

Evan Thomas's virtuosity was such that he could attract top New Orleans players to hop a train to the prairie and perform in the small towns of southwest Louisiana. In addition to Bunk Johnson, Harold Potier and Morris Dauphine, the Black Eagle lineup include other jazz luminaries like George Lewis, Joseph "Kid" Avery, George "Pop" Hamilton, Sam Dutrey Jr., Earl Humphrey, Abbey "Chinee" Foster and Chester Zardis.[84]

Perhaps it was Bunk Johnson who told Thomas of how Buddy Bolden used to "call his people home" by blowing his horn out the window to attract an audience. Dauphine called the practice "ballyhooing."

At that time, that was called ballyhooing around here. They would put the band on the back of a flat-bed truck and drive around with the music blastin'. They wouldn't announce the dance.…There was no television and very few people could afford a radio. If we were going to play, let's say in Franklin. OK? No advertisement…no nothing. We would go into town around five in the evening and head straight to the hall where we would set up our instruments on the back of a truck. When everything was ready the driver would take off with us playing our really hot numbers. He knew exactly where to go. We'd play a number here, play a number there and so on. Then the truck would end up back at the hall where we started. That night we would have a packed house.[85]

Bunk Johnson (trumpet) and George Lewis (clarinet) were rediscovered by jazz enthusiasts in the late 1930s who were interested in hearing what jazz sounded like at its inception. Johnson and Lewis were on the stage in Rayne's Promised Land when trumpeter Evan Thomas was murdered. Lewis felt the murderer's hand on his shoulder as Thomas was stabbed. Johnson's trumpet was destroyed, but Lewis, holding his clarinet with one hand, managed to get away and stow his clarinet. He escaped the assassin's second bandstand attack, this time with a shotgun, by diving through an open window. *William P. Gottlieb Collection, Library of Congress.*

Harold Potier said Evan would get to the gig early and "decide he didn't have anything to do so he would sit in the window of the club or hall where he was playing and blow his trumpet and drink. And do you know that night there would be a full house."[86]

Bunk and Evan meshed, said Lewis. "We took Bunk on as a second trumpet. He and Evan started soundin' real nice together—man, we *had* us a band then."[87]

Maybe it was the drinking that led to John Guillory and Evan Thomas's November 21 altercation. Thomas had re-formed the Black Eagles and had an extended tour of the southwestern United States and Mexico lined up. George Lewis on clarinet, Chinee Foster on drums, Bunk Johnson on second trumpet—the outlook was promising.[88] The first stop of the tour was set for Thomas's Crowley hometown, but at the last minute, he scheduled a paid rehearsal gig in the Promised Land neighborhood, a "negro residential section" of Rayne, only six miles away from Crowley.[89]

On the night of the gig, before Thomas arrived, several of the band members discovered John Guillory's house as a source for bootleg liquor. A pint was bought, and the drinkers went behind a wooden shack across the

Early jazz bands in New Orleans, Baton Rouge and small towns practiced the long-standing tradition of the "ballyhoo" by hiring a mule-driven wagon to carry the performing musicians, including a "tailgate" trombone, to make stops at saloons and cafés to advertise their evening show. This photo of Papa Jack Laine's Reliance Band, circa 1900, is the earliest known photo of a ballyhoo wagon. Laine was an early bandleader who served as an informal booking agent for musicians in New Orleans. *New Orleans Jazz Museum.*

street from the dance hall to partake. John Guillory, who had been recently released from the Louisiana State Penitentiary in Angola after serving a year for theft, was still "sporting fresh wounds he received in a knife attack by a woman."[90]

It's not clear who was drinking, but Thomas[91] and Bunk Johnson had a reputation for partaking.

"He [Johnson] was a drinking man," Harold Potier said. "We all drink and we're all not the same person when we get drunk. When Bunk was drinking, he was *drinking*."[92]

Dauphine added, "If he was drinking before a dance you might have to leave without him."[93]

Regardless of who was drinking the bootleg whiskey, when it was gone, the drinkers went back to Guillory's house and offered to buy more on credit. Presumably they would pay Guillory after the gig, when they were flush with cash. Guillory knew drunks and refused to sell on credit.

The *Rayne Tribune* published a front-page story of the Evan Thomas murder on November 27, 1931. The account characterized Thomas as a bandleader but also used his race as an identifier. The story said he expired on the steps of a nearby residence, but others say the Catholic Thomas died on the steps of a church. *From the* Rayne Acadian-Tribune, *Rayne, Louisiana.*

Perhaps upset with being cut off, one of the band members decided to insult Guillory and let it slip that Evan Thomas had carried on a relationship with Guillory's wife while he was away doing time.[94] Mable Young, Guillory's wife, was described by Banner Band trumpeter Harold Potier of Parks as "a beautiful woman,"[95] but he suspected she was something more than just beautiful. "She was one of those…movable women," Potier said.[96]

A band member told Thomas what happened with Guillory, and maybe it would have been wise to cut and run, but the show must go on. The Black Eagle Band took the stage and soon got a request, possibly from Guillory, to play "I'll Be Glad When You're Dead." George Lewis spotted Guillory approaching the bandstand, a large deer-hoof knife strapped to his side.

Guillory jumped on stage and exchanged angry words with Thomas. As Guillory slapped Thomas across the face, he reached for the knife. Lewis and two others, Bill Mouton and Arthur Crandall Jr., tried to disarm Guillory, and Thomas broke free and made for the door. Mouton and Crandall were both wounded by Guillory's blade.[97]

George Lewis never got John Guillory's name correct and called him "Gilbey" in his account of the slaughter.

Guillory/Gilbey come runnin' into the dance hall with a butcher knife. Said Evan been messin' around with his wife. Evan didn't have no time to run, so he grabbed me by the shoulders and ducked down behind me. Man I thought I was finished then. That man reached over me with that big knife and started hackin' at Evan. His wrist kept hittin' my shoulder. Blood was pourin out all over me. Cut Evan's throat. Then Guillory ran out of the hall, screamin' and cussin'.

We didn't have no time [to run]. It all happened so fast. After Guillory run out, I packed up my horn and put it behind the bandstand. Man, I was shakin'.…Pretty soon, Guillory run back in the hall with a shotgun, and I jumped headfirst out the window. Everybody scattered. Then he ments [commenced] with that gun, pickin' 'em up started blowin' holes in the instruments and throwin' 'em on the ground. Slashed the drumheads with his knife. Man, he went good and crazy. Wrecked Bunk's cornet for good. Bunk never played no more until we made those records [in 1942]. Everybody's instrument but mine was busted. And I have that clarinet case, yet.[98]

Potier, who was supposed to play saxophone that night, had a conflicting gig on trumpet and didn't play, but his secondhand report indicated Thomas had a slim chance to get away.

The man was coming on Evan with one of those deer foot knives. When Evan saw him, he ran, tried to get out of his way. If the door would have opened to the outside instead of the inside, Evan might have gotten away from him. But he had to open the door and pull it back. He still got out the building though. He ran about a block and died on the steps of a church. He died on the steps of a church.[99]

Guillory wasn't through, however. He left the hall briefly but returned with a shotgun. As Lewis mentioned, he shot up the bandstand, destroying Bunk's horn and all the other instruments he could find. Lewis's clarinet was only spared because he had the presence of mind to grab it before he abandoned the stage.[100]

The November 27, 1931 *Rayne Tribune* reported Guillory's stabbing blow "was driven with such force that it completely cut one of the victim's ribs in two."[101] Deputy Sheriff Gossen arrived on the scene and "sharply commanded him to drop [the gun] or he would be forced to kill him."[102] Guillory surrendered.

"Evan was a good Catholic," Harold Potier lamented.

There's a sad irony that Evan Thomas, the best trumpet player of the Louisiana southwest, died a gruesome death in the Promised Land on the steps of a church.[103]

Guillory's arrest and subsequent murder conviction were not the end of the story. Harold Potier, asked to perform on saxophone that night with Thomas, took a trumpet playing gig elsewhere. Potier took it as a sign to concentrate on the trumpet. It was a wise move for him. When he was drafted into the army in 1942, he played trumpet with the 418th Armed Forces Band overseas, which gave him the opportunity to play with top-notch musicians of diverse backgrounds. He toured New Zealand, Australia, India, Iran, Egypt and Italy.[104]

Bunk Johnson was shaken by the incident and had no money to replace his horn. His ability to perform was greatly reduced, and he had to borrow a trumpet to make any gig. He also lost his two front teeth, and he continued to drink. When he did get a gig, either on trumpet or tuba, he had to tie string across his remaining teeth to form an embouchure. Fortunately, in 1937, jazz researchers rediscovered Bunk and arranged to get him a set of false teeth and a new horn, and he was finally recorded.[105]

Guillory, convicted of the Thomas murder, was returned to Angola, where he behaved and achieved trustee status.[106] After a little more than three years of incarceration, he escaped. Although he was sighted in New Orleans, Houston and Beaumont, he managed to remain free for nearly a year.[107]

Not inexplicably, he returned to Rayne in September 1936 to see Mable Young, "the woman [who] had caused the trouble between Evan Thomas and Guillory when Thomas was playing for a dance here."[108] That's where he was identified exiting the Rosedale Gardens, a bar for white patrons. Guillory's skin tone was very light and could pass for white. He would have probably gone unnoticed in the bar except as he was leaving, another patron, Elias Faulk, who was entering, identified him and called the authorities. Night officer Donnie Ousse responded and approached Guillory, who was leaning on a vehicle across the street chatting with two friends and Mable Young. As Ousse approached, Guillory drew a long knife and slashed Ousse across the chest. Ousse managed to shoot Guillory three times, and the escaped convict died at the scene. Ousse, whose wounds were not considered serious at first, died a few days later.[109]

Had not Evan Thomas decided to take a practice gig, had not liquor been involved, had not Mable Young been a "movable woman,"[110] the modern audience might have been able to compare his sound with the other great trumpet players of the twentieth century. It's our loss.

Chapter 2

MUSICIANS, MURDERERS
AND MAYHEM

The 1920s were the heyday of the traveling musician. As part of the Great Migration, musicians from Louisiana were traveling not only within the state but also north to Memphis, St. Louis and Chicago; west to Los Angeles and San Francisco; and east to New York and Philadelphia.

And why not travel? The third generation of slave descendants had three choices: stay on the farm and continue to chop cotton and sugar cane; learn a trade; or move to the city.

"On the plantation you didn't see anything but sugarcane and corn," early jazz string bassist Pops Foster noted.[111] Foster was raised in the plantation community of McCall in Ascension Parish.

Louisiana was a wondrous and terrifying place during the early years of the twentieth century. Trains like the Smoky Mary, Southern Pacific Line and Great Northern[112] could ferry travelers around urban centers from New Orleans to Milneburg, West End and beyond. A train traveled across the Atchafalaya Swamp Basin, but the tracks were washed out during the flood of 1927. Radio stations began to broadcast entertainment, news and commercial messages to the masses. As Pappy O'Daniel famously says in *O, Brother Where Art Thou?*, "We ain't one-at-a-timin' here. We're mass communicating!"[113]

Musicians like Papa Celestin, born in Napoleonville, often traveled to Baton Rouge to play gigs. Excursion steamboats plied the waters of the Mississippi River, which brought a young Louis Armstrong to Baton

Rouge and later to St. Louis. The young Dippermouth, as he had come to be known, likely made his first appearance in the capital city probably two years before his first documented appearance with Fate Marable's Palmetto Jazzerites on the Streckfus steamboat *Capitol* in 1920.[114] Marable was the Streckfus bandleader and mentored many New Orleans musicians. Baton Rouge clarinetist Joe Darensbourg said he often heard Armstrong as he marched in funeral bands and parades.

"Everybody just all we could talk about was Louis Armstrong," Darensbourg remembered. "We called him Louis. And I said, Well, I'm going to play with that guy one of these days."[115]

If Darensbourg did predict a future playing with Armstrong, he prophesied well. Darensbourg, born on July 9, 1906, had a long and successful career as a clarinetist. He used a "slap tonguing" technique, the sound made when the tongue executes a spitting motion off the end of the tongue and creates a suction between the tongue and reed,[116] to propel his 1958 hit record with "Yellow Dog Blues"[117] onto the charts.

And he did play with Pops and his All Stars from 1961 to 1963. He was the clarinet player on Satchmo's 1963 number-one hit "Hello, Dolly."[118] "Dolly" dethroned the Beatles from the number-one spot on the *Billboard* charts.

Darensbourg said there were plenty of opportunities for musicians listed in trade magazines. "In those days, if you could play and wanted a job, all you'd do was get *Billboard*," Darensbourg said. "There was pages of jobs: medicine-show jobs, circus jobs, even boat jobs, minstrel shows, stock-company shows that played under canvas, regular road-house jobs, and bands organizing that wanted musicians."[119]

Growing up in Baton Rouge, he learned the shoemaking trade (a skill the Darensbourg family still practices in Louisiana's capital city), but shoe repair wasn't on young Joe's agenda. He had a wanderlust and fulfilled every American kid's dream: he ran off to join the circus.

"John Ringling of the Ringling Brothers Circus was a friend of my father's," Darensbourg said.[120]

But there were mixed results. His father would find out and send for him. He'd run away again.

"Actually, I didn't so much want to be a musician when I was a kid as I wanted to be a performer," he said. "If only we'd had someone to teach us, I'd probably have been a big-time circus performer instead of a lousy clarinet player."[121]

The third time Joe ran off with the circus, he made it to Los Angeles and wintered over. But this time, his father figured the boy could make it

Clarinetist Joe Darensbourg of Baton Rouge, born in 1906, learned the shoemaking trade from his father but left home for Opelousas to perform with the Martel Family Band. Darensbourg, later a member of Louis Armstrong's All Stars, had the dubious distinction to encounter two serial murderers, one in 1924 in Ville Platte, Louisiana, and the other in 1926 in Harrisburg, Illinois. *New Orleans Jazz Museum*.

back on his own when he got tired of living hand to mouth. He made it back to Baton Rouge by begging his cousin for the fare. He could have been a shoemaker or even a bricklayer, but Joe said the tradesmen worked the young guys too hard.

"These contractors are going to get all the labor out of you for nothing before they teach you," Darensbourg said. "You could learn actually laying bricks in two or three months, but they wouldn't allow that. Anyway, when I got through fooling with them goddam bricks I was too tired to go see Mable….And my cousin Theodore was making time with her….So I said to hell with it."[122]

In 1922, unhappy with the prospect of being a shoemaker or bricklayer and unlucky in love, young Joe decided music was his best chance of personal fulfillment. "I got my clarinet for real then," he wrote.[123]

The path he chose ultimately proved successful, but it was filled with detours and life-threatening physical setbacks. Darensbourg couldn't predict the violence he'd encounter on the road, but he wasn't a stranger to brutal behavior in his hometown. He recalled Jim Bernard's restaurant on Liberty Street (now South Twelfth Street) specialized in oyster loaves, chicken loaves, red beans and rice, French bread and possum and sweet potatoes.[124]

"Jim Bernard was a resourceful guy, so he figured out a clever idea to tell people whenever he got a couple of possums," Darensbourg said. "He rigged up a steam whistle on top of his place, like a train, and when he had possum and sweet potatoes he'd give it three toots. Everybody in Baton Rouge got so that they knew that whistle, and when they heard it, guys would be running from every part of town."[125]

The cook, nicknamed Crackshot, was a cantankerous sort and mouthed off to the wrong customer who complained the chef shorted his share of the possum. Crackshot brained the man with an iron skillet. Enraged, the customer pulled out a .45, known as a "Saturday Night Harrison," put it up to Crackshot's forehead and fired. Crackshot crumpled to the floor, but the cartridge was defective and lodged only partly in the cook's forehead. Crackshot was only down for an eight count, and by the time Doc Murray arrived on the scene, he was up on his feet complaining.

"My head is hurtin'. I gotta headache," said Crackshot.[126]

The bleeding stopped, and the slug, the circumference of a silver dime, protruded from his forehead.

"Somebody went and got some sandpaper and Doc Murray started to level that bullet off," Darensbourg reported. "Crackshot just left it there and eventually he had it monogrammed 'C.S.' for Crackshot."[127]

In 1923, Darensbourg left Baton Rouge to join the Martel Family Band of Opelousas, a St. Landry Parish town about sixty miles from Baton Rouge.

"They was playing jazz," Darensbourg said. "They was playing 'Tiger Rag' and 'Sister Kate' and all those tunes. Hillary Martel played banjo and some piano and her father, old man Albert Martel, played a B-flat soprano sax. I started playing with them and who was in that band but Manuel Manetta and Barney's brother, Alex Bigard."[128]

The Martels' musicianship was good but not great, with one exception.

"None of them was outstanding musicians but old man Martel was damn good on that saxophone," Darensbourg said. "They might have been better if they'd left there, but they was like some others that didn't ever want to leave home. A lot of these young guys won't leave home, or they're afraid to leave the security of home."[129]

Darensbourg impregnated Hillary Martel, ten years his senior, so he married her and settled in Opelousas for a while. He got a side job in Chapman's Shoe Shop.[130] In southwest Louisiana, he was exposed to the musicianship of Bunk Johnson, Evan Thomas ("He was out of this world, great! He made a trumpet sound like a violin."),[131] the Blue Devils of Plaquemine and the Black Eagle Band from Crowley.

Darensbourg, a person of color, had a fair complexion and could have played with white bands and made more money. "I could see the injustice of the race thing. I had guys saying I was crazy to be fooling around with these colored guys," Joe said. "[But] I'd much rather play with these fellows 'cause the colored guys just had it."[132]

As a result, he was subject to the discrimination suffered by Black people in rural Louisiana as the Martel Band played in small French-speaking towns like Plaisance, Big Mamou, Little Mamou[133] and Chataignier at Guillory's Hall[134] and Fontenot's Hall.[135] And the Ku Klux Klan was still playing a role in Louisiana politics and elsewhere in the early 1920s. The newspapers were filled with articles decrying Ku Klux Klan attempts to influence elections, and it got so bad that Governor John M. Parker outlawed Klan parades.[136] Klan national membership in the 1920s rose ominously to more than five million.[137]

Joe related the type of harassment bands could encounter in the South:

Some of those southern people are the cruelest people in the world. One of the things they would do was to block off a road when a band was traveling home. They never did stop the Martels because old man Martel was a kinda tough character, but they'd make the black bands stop and have them play until they felt like letting them leave. Usually there'd be nothing but one little old dirt road to get out of town, so you was trapped. I remember another musician telling me about a band which had played a dance, got through about one o'clock in the morning, and the crackers got them on the outskirts of town. They seen this bunch of lights and a circle of cars, and these guys stopped the band, made them take out their instruments and play right out there on the road for nothing. It happened to me one time when I was with a white band out of Memphis when we was in Mississippi. Makes you ashamed to be white. You had more good white people than you had bad, otherwise there wouldn't have been a Black man alive, but some of them would kill colored people for the fun of it. You ask where the term "alligator bait" comes from, and that's where they'd cut the eyes out and use them as bait. All kinds of cruel things. [138]

Black people in Louisiana, especially traveling Black musicians, tried to be as deferential to whites as possible and were familiar with the concept of the "laughing barrel,"[139] apocryphal or not. "You'd be walking around one of these towns and probably somebody made a remark or seen something funny, enough to make you want to laugh real loud. You had to go stick your head in the barrel and mute that sound. They had them all down South…. This was just done to Black guys to show them who was boss. Those people were bastards," Darensbourg reported.[140]

Darensbourg also recalled playing a gig in Shreveport and how "we saw all these people standing on a dirt road, out of town, and we wondered what it was. Turned out they had lynched a colored guy, put a big chain around his neck and drug him around town, right past a colored school."

Young Darensbourg and the Martel Band also experienced proper courtroom justice in action when they were in the Ville Platte area for a two-night stand and among the crowd that witnessed "the first legal hanging in the parish"[141] on August 8, 1924.

No matter how tough old man Martel was, his musicians wisely made note of Klan mention in the media. But what did they make of the front page of the April 30, 1921 *St. Landry Clarion* of Opelousas? Were they shocked when they read, "Waylay, Shoots and Mortally Wounds Evangeline Farmer?"[142] in which it was reported that Pierre Vidrine, a "respectable citizen"[143] and farmer in rural Turkey Creek, was ambushed? The same front page had news of a "giant Black" suspected murderer captured in Allen Parish,[144] a shooting suicide of an Opelousas man[145] and the deaths of two white men in a shotgun duel in Pointe Coupee Parish.[146] Was it just a bad week for the Cajun prairie?

As for the first headline, Pierre Vidrine, a seventy-year-old farmer,[147] was found dead in his fields nearly torn in two by shotgun blasts.[148] Suspicion fell on the French-speaking Euzebe Vidrine, a twenty-year-old farmer, because there was bad blood between the two unrelated men. The *St. Landry Clarion* reported that young Euzebe had a run-in at a *bal de maison* (house dance) hosted by Pierre.[149] Pierre's dog had killed some of Euzebe's sheep, so Euzebe killed the dog. In retaliation, Pierre spread the rumor that Euzebe was a "hog stealer."[150] Deputy Fontenot also located a single-barrel shotgun of "cheap make" with the initials "E.V." carved in the stock.[151] Euzebe was arrested and jailed for thirty days because he could not make bail.[152]

"They made a warrant against me and Mr. Lee Andrus because we were the only ones in the community who had not offered assistance," Euzebe said.[153]

When Judge B.H. Pavy's grand jury convened, he lamented there was no bloodhound kennel available in the parish to track "to earth the cowardly perpetrators of these dastardly crimes."[154]

Euzebe was put on trial less than two months after Pierre's death, but District Attorney Lee Garland could not convince the jury because "the evidence submitted was purely circumstantial, not sufficiently strong to convict…and the accused was acquitted."[155]

Euzebe went back to his own farm at Turkey Creek, but something was off with the young farmer. As a teenager, he was prone to crying jags.[156] He had wept for three days in the privacy of his home[157] after being accused of stealing pigs. There were other stressors. His father died when Euzebe was nineteen, and his brother was killed in a fight. He had bad luck with his plow horses and shot and killed his mule out of frustration because he could not pen it into the harness.[158] He and his young wife, Lillian Andrus, separated. Lillian found work as a cashier in a New Iberia café, while the depressed Euzebe looked for work in Lafayette, Shreveport and Monroe.[159] By then, Euzebe had murdered two innocent men.

"I never said anything about my hard luck; but I had a good idea why I was so unlucky; it was because I had done so much meanness to other people; never believed much in religion; never obeyed God," wrote Euzebe. "I was despondent, disgusted and disappointed enough to commit suicide, but instead I made up my mind that I was going to kill people on the road for a living."[160]

THE LIFE OF
EUZEBE VIDRINE

...Published By...
AURELIS MAYEAUX
V. L. DUPUIS
J. HUGO DORE, Trustees.
Ville Platte, La.
"COPYRIGHT 1924"   All Rights Reserved

Euzebe Vidrine murdered five men over a three-year period in Louisiana and Texas in 1921–24. Caught after killing the Evangeline Parish sheriff's son, he penned *The Life of Euzebe Vidrine*, "a unique record of crime," while in jail as he awaited hanging. *LSU Special Collections.*

On December 2, 1921, he shot taxi driver Charles Garbo of Lafayette.

"I went to a colored man as I preferred to kill a negro than a white man [and] asked if he could take me to Kaplan," Euzebe said. "I was just itching to kill. I could feel the devil urging me on, so I shot him in the head with a 32-caliber pistol."[161]

He killed a second cab driver, J.B. Roy of Crowley, near Eunice, a St. Landry Parish town about forty miles from Lafayette, on December 3. Euzebe described Roy as a "half-breed Mexican."[162]

"He had a swell pocket book and a cheap watch," Euzebe noted. "I opened up the pocket book. I found sand; gravel was wrapped up with little rags, and one nickel in the center. It was his 'hoodoo.' I threw everything away except the nickel."[163]

Authorities thought the murders of Roy and Garbo were connected, but no arrests were made.[164] On December 13, less than two weeks later, a third jitney driver, Lee Duke, forty-five, was found murdered near Orange, Texas, with a bullet wound to the "brain cavity."[165] Euzebe kept Duke's watch, which was engraved with his initials.[166] Upon his return to Ville Platte, he was questioned by the Lafayette Parish sheriff but not arrested. Euzebe filed Duke's initials off the watch after the confrontation.

Unlike in the Louisiana cab driver murders, Texas authorities arrested[167] and convicted Frank Smith[168] for the murder of Duke. They got the wrong man.

Smith might have stayed in jail if Euzebe Vidrine could have controlled his compulsion to kill, but hard luck followed the young couple wherever they went. They tried to farm in Evangeline Parish in 1922, but Lillian, a product of the 1920s "mass culture that challenged the ruling norms of womanhood,"[169] missed city life and left him. The abandoned farm was sold by Sheriff R.L. Wiggins at a tax sale in April 1922.[170] Euzebe went to Hot Springs, Arkansas, where he was arrested and jailed for a short while on an illegal gun possession charge. He then left for Monroe, Louisiana, and later found work in Gibsland, Louisiana, site of the 1934 Bonnie and Clyde ambush.[171] He was held by Arcadia authorities for vagrancy and then found work in a carbon plant in Swartz in Ouachita Parish and the paper mill in Bastrop (Morehouse Parish). He accumulated some money, bought a suit on credit with a false name from Pollach Clothing Company and sent for Lillian. She looked for work in Bastrop but left him again after he refused to give her money and moved to Shreveport. Euzebe decided to return to Ville Platte and considered "black-handing"[172] planter Numa Morein by writing a letter to him threatening harm.[173] He also bought another suit on credit in Alexandria from Pollach Clothing and bilked them again.

His family, ignorant of Euzebe's murderous activity, welcomed him home. He stayed with his mother and repaired her house. He decided to farm there. But his conscience bothered him.

"I had plenty of good clothes and had saved about one hundred dollars; my people were so happy. I envied them. I felt I was the most miserable creature in existence," he wrote.[174]

Sheriff Wiggins, the man who had arrested Euzebe Vidrine in 1921, was in Baton Rouge on May 19, 1924, attending Governor Henry L. Fuqua's inauguration when he was notified that his son Robert Leo Wiggins had been murdered on the road between Mamou and Ville Platte. Young Wiggins's Ford coupe was found bogged down in a gully 150 yards off the road "halfway between Mrs. Thomas Vidrine's and the Baskin Fontenot bridge on Bayou Joe Manuel [Bayou Jos Marcel]."[175] An eyewitness saw a young man "step from the car and walk away into the woods."[176] The still warm body of Leo Wiggins was found under a nearby oak tree.[177]

Euzebe, hiding in the woods, went into town to establish an alibi. Standing at the corner of the Evangeline Bank building, he witnessed Wiggins's body sprawled out in the back seat of a "large Buick car"[178] as it was being brought in for examination and dressing. Euzebe jumped on the vehicle's running board and got a good look.[179]

Possibly as a feigned show of respect, he visited the coroner's home where the body was taken and asked, "Which one of Sheriff Wiggins' boys were killed?"[180] The gathering crowd, in the mood for a lynching, suspected Euzebe, but Sheriff Wiggins warned against it. Evidence, however, quickly piled up against the melancholy Euzebe Vidrine.

The *Weekly Gazette* reported that a "blood-stained shoe, clothing worn by Euzebe Vidrine, a .32 caliber pistol, a score of cartridges, the bullets corresponding to those fired into Leo Wiggins, one being found under his shirt when the body was being dressed"[181] were found in Euzebe's room. The black-hand letter to Numa Morein was also found.[182] He was arrested and brought to jail as a suspect.[183]

And then there were the dogs…

Judge Pavy wished bloodhounds had been available during the 1921 Pierre Vidrine murder investigation. With the Wiggins murder, authorities sent for Bob Gant of Mississippi and his pack of bloodhounds. Coroner Yves Ardoin, the father-in-law of the victim, put Leo's Ford coupe under guard[184] so the crime scene was minimally contaminated. The *St. Landry Clarion* reported:

> *The dogs arrived Tuesday night, and took up the trail from the coupe, which had been carefully guarded by Officers of Evangeline. The hounds went right into Ville Platte, passing over the identical route used by Vidrine, into a pool room, where he had played a game of pool, to the home of Dr. Ardoin and then to the bank corner, where Vidrine was alleged to have alighted in an automobile the night of the killing. The dogs then lost the trail. They were brought near the jail and quickly picked up the scent and went right to Vidrine's cell yelping as they saw him. Vidrine is alleged to have fainted.*[185]

Euzebe did not confirm whether the bloodhounds proved his guilt, but his mental anguish reached a breaking point, and he confessed to the murders of Robert Leo Wiggins, Pierre Vidrine, Charles Garbo, John Roy and Lee Duke.[186]

Thousands of people arrived in Ville Platte to watch the public execution of Euzebe—so many that the courthouse fence was knocked down by the throng. Reporters from the *Times-Picayune* and *New Orleans Item* covered the trial and subsequent hanging,[187] and their stories were picked up by the regional newspapers, the *New York Times*[188] and nationally by *Time* magazine.[189]

Euzebe posed for a photographer on his way to the gallows chatting with Sheriff Charles Pucheu and posed again for a shot with the noose around his neck. *Time* reported, "At Ville Platte, La., one Euzebe Vidrine, about to be hanged for murder, asked permission to make a speech to the spectators, began in English, stumbled, went on for thirty minutes in French. Said he: 'Do not gamble. Do not drink whiskey.'"[190] His last words were, "Cut it, Charley, and be my friend."

The best account of the spectacle came from the editor of Ville Platte's *Weekly Gazette*, aka the "Little Old Man" (J. Emile Pucheu). It captures French Louisiana perfectly:

AND THEN—DEATH.—Without the flicker of a lash, Euzebe Vidrine, who slew five men, stood while Sheriff Charles Pucheu adjusted the noose in Ville Platte, La. The sheriff was the more nervous of the two. "Courage, Charlie—cut the rope and set me free," he said. "Leave bad whisky, women, pistols alone. Think of God and mother and all will be well," were his last words. Then Charlie sprang trap.

The "first legal hanging in Evangeline Parish," a public execution of multiple murderer Euzebe Vidrine, made national headlines in 1924. Vidrine addressed the crowd gathered for the spectacle in French, his first language. The troubled man's message was simple: "Do not gamble. Do not drink whiskey." *From the* Daily News, *New York.*

They were here in thousands, these French-Americans of this southland Arcadie; "from the far corners of the Parish of Evangeline named for Longfellow's maid of sorrows." They were here from everywhere, gathered in the dusty streets, filling the courtyard, standing alongside the stockade built on the east side of the jail house. They talked their French or the patois that compromises with English. They were excited; it is their nature to be excited even over small things, but this, the solemn taking of a man's life, is no small thing. When whispers from those nearest the stockade carried the word "the sheriff has just cut the rope," they tarried for a brief half hour in conversation; talked over the crime; told how they heard the trap fall that shot the soul of Euzebe Vidrine into eternity. Their vengeance sated, they turned their steps homeward thinking on the way not of "Euzebe," as all spoke of him, but Madame Vidrine—the mother of a son who sowed to the wind.[191]

But Euzebe got the final word. While in jail, Euzebe, with the help of his trustees, Aurelis Mayeaux, V.L. Dupuis and J. Hugo Doré, wrote "an eloquent flow of words"[192] about his life, marriage and accounts of the murders. The detail was important because it secured the release of Frank Smith, who was unjustly convicted of Lee Duke's murder in Texas.[193] Messiers Mayeaux, Dupuis and Doré were probably responsible for the sporadic injection of verse from Charles Kingsley, Omar Khayyám and Fitz-Greene Halleck[194] in the thirty-five-page volume, as Euzebe had only finished the fourth grade and French was his first language. The book sold for one dollar and was advertised in the Opelousas and Lafayette newspapers.[195] The Little Old Man was opposed to Euzebe's estate profiting from his life of crime and editorialized, "If the 'sins' in the issuance of Vidrine's life of crime was at public uplift, moral welfare, then its projectors should circulate it FREE— not commercialize it for filthy lucre,"[196] but his newspaper ran the ad as well.

Did Joe Darensbourg and the Martel Band play a gig that Euzebe Vidrine attended? Joe said the Martels played in Ville Platte every week, so it's possible. Euzebe said he learned to be a good dancer, and his family would go to "the dance" on Saturday night.[197] Euzebe knew his music too and requested the "Dying Millions" hymn at his final jailhouse service.[198]

And even though it was Prohibition, there was plenty of 200-proof moonshine available to Euzebe. He even tried his hand at liquor-making but stayed drunk most of the time. Euzebe said liquor brought him to the gallows. Darensbourg said the gallows were built directly across the street from the dance hall, and he and his band members saw the whole thing from the hall's rooftop.

Darensbourg's telling of the Euzebe Vidrine story in his autobiography got some basic facts wrong, but it's certain he viewed the hanging. He was also one of thousands who passed by Vidrine's open coffin, put on view at Euzebe's request.[199] And Darensbourg's description of how he felt about the execution is visceral:

It made me sick the rest of the day to see him dropping through the trapdoor and hanging there, just swinging. It looked like it took him five minutes to die. Doctor walked up and put a stethoscope to his heart. When they cut him down, they had him laid out there so you could see his face. His face was black, and his tongue was hanging out. Yet the people was there with their kids on their shoulders so they could see it better. I know I'll never forget it.[200]

Like in the rest of America, the Jazz Age in Louisiana was a time of change and turmoil. The country had fought in a terrible world war. English became the official language taught in Louisiana's public schools.[201] Women had gained the right to vote. Electric lines were being installed. Consumerism and mass media created sensationalism, and a cult of beauty led to the sexual objectification of women.[202] Radio became the "most immediate and ubiquitous outlet for the dissemination of news."[203]

No doubt the Frenchmen of Evangeline Parish were shocked by Euzebe's killings, but what degree of shock did they feel when they heard of Leopold and Loeb's "thrill kill" in June 1924, as reported by the local media?[204] What went through their collective mind when they learned that Euzebe confessed, "When I kill, it makes me rejoice?"[205] and "I don't know why I killed Leo Wiggins and the others. A feeling comes over me and I must kill somebody, anybody—then I felt better."[206]

The puzzled *Weekly Gazette* tried to assign motive to Euzebe's actions. Pierre Vidrine "talked too much." Charles Garbo was robbed. John Roy was robbed of a nickel. Lee Duke was robbed of seventy-five cents, a watch and a pistol. Leo Wiggins was robbed.[207] It must have been too shocking for the flappers of the Roaring Twenties to think of a concept as horrendous as a serial murderer.

Joe Darensbourg's take? "Some of those southern people are the cruelest people in the world."[208]

But Joe had not yet encountered Charlie Birger of Harrisburg, Illinois.

WHEN DARENSBOURG SAT DOWN with Peter Vacher and dictated *Jazz Odyssey: The Autobiography of Joe Darensbourg* to him, Vacher did not have the luxury of the Internet to verify the 1926 bombing of Charlie Birger's Shady Rest roadhouse. He just had Joe sitting in his living room chair in 1979 telling stories. Joe's memories were fifty years old, and Birger's crimes were forgotten by most of the American public.

You can't blame Vacher and Joe for the incorrect spelling of Birger and rival gangster Carl Shelton. But one thing Darensbourg nailed on the head about the gangs of Little Egypt, the nickname for southern Illinois: "Life didn't mean nothing to these guys. If you got in their way they killed you, that's all. That was a way of life with them. The thing was, nothing ever happened to them."[209]

That's not entirely true. Things did happen to them—bad things.

Darensbourg encountered the Birger gang as he traveled with Doc Moon's Medicine Show. "They must have had two dozen minstrel shows in those days and they was always through Opelousas," Darensbourg said.[210]

Along the way on the Doc Moon gig, Joe encountered white minstrels Neil O'Brien, Honey Melody and Al G. Fields and the blackface white comedians Moran and Mack perform as the Two Black Crows and the Sam and Henry actors who became the Amos 'n' Andy comedy team, but they "didn't compare with the natural black actors."[211] He also encountered the great Black blues singers Ma Rainey, Chippie Hill, Mamie Smith and Bessie Smith.

"They tell me she [Bessie Smith] was a pretty good drinker," Joe related. "It's true she drank all the time."[212]

The ballyhoo for minstrel shows and medicine shows were very similar. The show's band, always wearing nice uniforms, paraded into the town alongside some of the performers. Darensbourg said the drummers had a show of their own, and the greatest of them all was a man named Manzie Campbell of the Florida Blossom Minstrels. "He was the first street drummer I ever seen juggling his sticks while he was marching," said Joe.[213]

A specially equipped railroad car carried Doc Moon's gear and was set off on a sidetrack in the rail yard. The promoting parade would start there, proceed to the town square, perform a short concert and advertise the evening show.

"People in those small towns, the only time they ever heard any music or got any entertainment was when those minstrel shows or a medicine show, a circus or a carnival came through," Darensbourg said.

The night Doc Moon's Medicine Show came to Opelousas, Darensbourg was jamming on saxophone with a guitar player named Big Boy and a singer named Blue Coat. The sax was still a bit of a novelty horn in the 1920s, although Joe had played one with Toots Johnson's Baton Rouge band.[214] Big Boy invited Joe to saddle up with Doc Moon's band.

Joe was married to Martel's daughter and had put down some roots in Opelousas by taking a job with Boston Electric Shoe Shop.[215]

"Mr. Chapman almost cried when I left, no kidding," Darensbourg said. "He says, 'Joe, I want you to stay here.' He was going to make me a partner in the business."[216]

Darensbourg left the stability of life in Opelousas to play saxophone on the road with a flimflam medicine show. Joe didn't own a saxophone, so Doc Moon advanced him cash to get one.

"Doc was white and he wasn't a doctor—none of these guys was doctors—he just had a good line of bullshit," said Darensbourg.[217]

MOON'S TONIC

Thousands of satisfied users testify that Moon's Tonic is the most wonderful medicine for Kidney, Bladder, Stomach and Blood Troubles on the market. If troubled with backache, up and down during the night, constipation, indigestion or similar troubles, try it. As a Blood Purifier there is nothing to equal it. For sale by

Eldredge's Drug Store
And Druggists Everywhere
Address all orders:
Moon's Medicine Co., Box 296, Baton Rouge, La.

Joe Darensbourg traveled with the Baton Rouge–based Doc Moon's Medicine Show from Louisiana up to the "Little Egypt" region of southern Illinois. Along the way, they sold Moon's Tonic. "People in those small towns, the only time they ever heard any music or got any entertainment was when those minstrel shows or a medicine show, a circus or a carnival came through," Darensbourg said. *From the* Abbeville Meridional, *Abbeville, Louisiana.*

But Moon was well equipped. Joe was familiar with the Doc, a Baton Rouge resident. Darensbourg claimed Moon was a millionaire and owned a $30,000 travel bus with sleeping quarters and a medicine room with vats to mix and bottle the medicine. They'd hit a town, the bus bedecked with a banner, and ballyhoo the "Free Medicine Show with Moon's Medicine Show." The band featured Darensbourg on saxophone, two clarinets, a guitar, a female singer and a bass.

We put up a portable platform, no top over it. This was a first-class deal with a big stage, about the size of a room. Then we had these gas lights that you pump up and light.

Doc Moon would get up there and start his spiel…. "Look, I want you people to know that I'm not doing this to make money. I'm here because I love you people and I want to heal your suffering. If you think I'm here to make money off you, then I want you to get the hell off this lot right now. I don't need your money. I got money to throw away." Then he'd throw about three or four dollars into the audience. The people about killed each other trying to get it. Then he'd say, "Ok, the band will strike up a tune here and entertain us."[218]

Someone from the show would always go into the town and find the town bum, bandage him up, put him in a wheelchair and wheel him on stage. "So, this guy would be shaking and trembling like he was real sick," Darensbourg related.

Doc would then recite the man's forty years of illnesses. "'If my tonic can cure him…' You know the rest," Darensbourg said. "The bum would take a sip of the tonic and start dancing around the stage to 'Tiger Rag.' The bum would probably win an Academy Award for acting. Some of them were so real. Often the guy would only do it if Doc put real liquor in the bottle."[219]

Joe said most small towns welcomed the medicine shows, as they were a source of free entertainment. The *Weekly Iberian* reporter who covered the February 10, 1927 Moon Medicine Show wasn't taken in by the doctor's palaver but noted there were plenty who were.

"We were somewhat surprised to learn we had been born with ills we never knew we had, or existed, and the medicine would cure them, or money back. From the number of bottles sold the physicians can take a long vacation, for the epidemic of mumps will banish, we will have no more smallpox, or even cases of indigestion, or bruises will be cured in no time at all," the reporter concluded.[220]

The gigs were easy, about an hour long, Darensbourg said. When they sold out of tonic, the show was over. The show's marketing strategy meant visiting only the outskirts of larger towns to perform, and there was plenty of time for Moon's musicians to find side gigs. When they were in the St. Louis area, Darensbourg was able to play gigs on Fate Marable's riverboat excursions and with Charlie Creath's Jazz-o-Maniacs and Jelly Roll Morton. He even recorded with Creath on some sides for Okeh.[221]

Jazz Odyssey: The Autobiography of Joe Darensbourg has some factual errors, but Darensbourg was honest when he told his story, warts and all, to writer Peter Vacher. He liked to chase women, and he liked to drink and said, "We'd do anything to buy some liquor" during Prohibition.[222] Was it the love of music that brought Darensbourg to gangster Charlie Birger's Shady Rest roadhouse or the love of liquor?

Here's what Joe Darensbourg walked into.

Charlie Birger, accustomed to using violence, had been running whores, gambling houses and whiskey in the dry southern Illinois counties[223] for years before the Doc Moon show rolled into Harrisburg. Probably because of its proximity to Cairo, Illinois, that section of the state was known as "Little Egypt,"[224] and Birger, allied with the Shelton boys, aspired to be its pharaoh. Birger had probably already committed at least one murder and been exonerated in the killing of two others. He had also been shot and left for dead once but survived.[225]

Darensbourg might not have known the area was controlled by gangsters, but bassist Pops Foster, who was playing on the riverboats in the early 1920s, had heard rumors. "When we first started playing in St. Louis, we had some guys always standing around the bandstand," Foster said. "We didn't know who they were but later on we found out they were guards. The Streckfus people thought we might have some trouble with white musicians and the gangsters."[226]

Foster said the boat musicians never had trouble with gangsters. He believed the Streckfus management was keeping them away from roadhouse gigs.

In 1922, the Marion Law Enforcement League in Marion, Illinois, "considered by many to be synonymous with the Ku Klux Klan,"[227] arranged for a Prohibition agent named S. Glenn Young to crack down on bootleggers. Young was a controversial figure. He revived the Klan. He was accused of murder. His first wife divorced him on cruelty grounds, and he remarried within two weeks.[228] Young apologist E. Bishop Hill, twenty years old when he wrote *Complete History of Southern Illinois' Gang War*, said of the charismatic enforcer, "To his admirers he was a dauntless crusader who feared neither man nor the devil in fighting sin such as he found it in and around Herrin. To those who hated him, he was a swashbuckling interloper whose own violences were greater than the crimes he attempted to correct."[229]

Young, who previously arrested World War I draft dodgers, was overzealous from the start. After five months on the job, he shot and killed a bootlegging suspect in his home during a raid. Although he was acquitted, the federal agency fired Young. He then worked for two years in New Orleans with the Illinois Central Railroad. While he was down south, an Illinois labor riot caused the death of twenty-one striking and strike-breaking miners in the Herrin Massacre of June 21, 1922. Although 214 indictments were issued, no one was convicted.

Fearful that Little Egypt was now giving a "green light to criminals of every sort,"[230] the Marion Law Enforcement League (KKK) called up Young to recruit "hundreds of men"[231] to enforce the Volstead Act's liquor ban. Young administered dubious communal oaths to his recruits and set them out to execute federal search warrants on bootlegging operations. During the initial raid and subsequent searches, the so-called constables often overstepped their authority. It was common knowledge that the raiders were stealing personal property,[232] but the courts ruled that "these defendants who claim they were victims of spite work in the Ku Klux Klan raids…will have to prove…that any liquor found in the homes was there without their knowledge," wrote the *Murphysboro Daily Independent*.[233]

Young went too far when he called for the removal of Sheriff George Galligan in an investigation of the death of a Klan constable.[234] Galligan

S. Glenn Young was a "Prohis" (Prohibition agent) fired for excessive violence in a liquor raid in 1921. The Illinois Ku Klux Klan hired him in 1923 to lead Prohibition raids against illegal liquor possession that targeted bootleggers but also menaced ordinary citizens who wanted alcohol, including Italian and French Catholic immigrants. Young was eventually indicted on fifty-five counts of assault with intent to murder, conspiracy, kidnapping, false imprisonment, robbery, larceny and falsely assuming office. He was killed on January 24, 1925, in a shootout with Deputy Ora Thomas. The Klan violence led to a gang war that nearly killed Louisiana jazz musician Joe Darensbourg. *Marion, Illinois History Preservation.*

said he "objected to raids in which women and children were struck down, children hit over the heads with guns....Those that were beaten up with guns and the stealing of money and property which had engendered a bitter feeling."[235] Galligan called for federal troops to occupy the city because he did not want a repeat of the Herrin Massacre.[236]

But Galligan and the Herrin mayor were arrested, and Young took over as sheriff.[237]

Anti-Klan forces resisted during a February 8, 1924 raid on the Rome Club. Earl Shelton, then a Birger ally, had been roughed up in a previous Klan encounter. Shelton was cold cocked repeatedly by "prominent Klansman" Caesar Cagle.[238] Cagle, identified as a "constable" in the *Moline Daily Dispatch*,[239] was allegedly shot in the ear by Earl Shelton during the Rome Club raid as the gangsters went on a Klan-killing mission.[240] There were conflicting reports on who killed Cagle. The *Edwardsville Intelligencer* reported that "Cagle was shot four times, and his skull crushed in by savage blows with a blunt instrument according to S. Glenn Young."[241] Young claimed Deputy Ora Thomas, Earl and Carl Shelton and Sheriff Galligan were the four men who fired the shots that killed Cagle.[242]

Sheriff Galligan's deputy, John Layman, shot in the chest during the mêlée, was brought to Black Hospital, which came under siege the entire night by Klan forces. Twenty-one bullet holes were later counted in Layman's hospital room. Deputy Thomas came under fire by Klan shooters at Black Hospital while protecting Layman during the riot.

Young, a "paid employee of the Ku Klux Klan"[243] without a federal commission, was called to account for the violence in the "Rome Club Riot."[244] He was charged with fifty-five counts of "assault with intent to murder, conspiracy, kidnapping, false imprisonment, robbery, larceny and falsely assuming office."[245] He was killed eleven months later on January 24, 1925, in a shootout with Deputy Ora Thomas, a friend of the wounded Deputy Layman. Two of Young's bodyguards were also killed. Thomas, a former miner, may have believed the rumor that Young was a strikebreaker in the Herrin Massacre, a story Young vehemently denied, but Thomas had also been publicly insulted by Young several times. It was no secret the thirty-three-year-old Thomas was gunning for Young.[246]

His dying words were, "Did I get Young?"

"Yes," he was told.

"Then I am willing to die."[247]

To some, Young's death signaled the Klan war was over. Peace appeared to be sustained by Mississippi preacher Howard Williams's religious revival in June 1925, but Charlie Birger and the Sheltons had not forgotten their lost profits.

"The Ku Klux Klan began to stir things up in Herrin and Shelton and I began to tone down some of the Klansmen, although they got a bunch of our men too,"[248] Charlie Birger said.

There was a final burst of Klan-gangster violence in the aftermath of the April 1926 local elections that resulted in a decisive victory for Klan-backed candidates. The spark? A Klan poll watcher challenged several Catholic voters, one a nun who had been a Herrin resident for twenty years. Fistfights and shootings broke out, and when the smoke cleared, six people were dead. The Williamson County residents were weary of their "Bloody Williamson" reputation, and Klan harassment of the bootleggers ended.

Author Gary Deneal summed it up in his book *A Knight of Another Sort: Prohibition Days and Charlie Birger*:

The shock of the battle with its half dozen dead was of greatest concern.
Some realized that the Ku Klux Klan could not withstand the machine guns
of the gangsters. What had begun as an idealistic crusade by ministers had
degenerated into an exercise in destruction and general lawlessness under the
leadership of S. Glenn Young.[249]

Bootleggers, labor violence, coal miners, the Ku Klux Klan, fascism, rapid technological changes—Doc Moon may have known what Little Egypt was all about when he brought his medicine show there, but what experience did the mixed-race, nineteen-year-old Joe Darensbourg have? He had already left behind a promising trade, abandoned his wife and infant son and was stealing Doc Moon's product and selling it on the side.[250] How would Little Egypt treat this talented but naïve clarinet player?

Regarding ladies, Joe had no trouble. He met a sixteen-year-old girl named Ruby in Centralia. Ruby's father worked for the railroad and was gone for days at a time. Darensbourg would whistle the "Sleepy Time Gal" melody when he was outside her home, and she'd shimmy down the porch post if the coast was clear. Ruby's father got tipped off to the musical cue.

"Apparently he got wind of his daughter fooling with one of these medicine-show fellows and he was waiting for me," Darensbourg said. "When I hit 'Sleepy Time Gal' that front door flew open, and he rushed out of there with a baseball bat. The race was on. I had my saxophone case in my hand and, believe me, I set some world records that night."[251]

Darensbourg admitted he liked to drink and could easily find liquor in St. Louis. There was a procedure to procure a drink. At a location near the Booker T. Washington Theater, a fellow had an operation on the second floor. A cup equipped with a bell was hung from the upper window. A customer would ring to signal and put in his own bottle and a buck for the "mickey." "That's what they called a half-pint," Darensbourg said.[252]

That method was okay for the urban areas, but it was trickier in rural Illinois.

"You had a lot of guys bootlegging," he said. "There was this farm where they used to make moonshine and we'd go out there in an old open Ford, usually at night. It had to be three guys if you was going to buy a couple of gallons at a time."[253]

The musicians were always wary. Darensbourg related:

Revenu-ers…[were] government men that was trying to catch you with
liquor and put you in jail, but they had to catch you with the evidence. In
order to be sure the Revenue-ers wouldn't catch us with the evidence if they

stopped us, one of us would be sitting each side of the car with a gallon jug suspended outside with a hammer in our hands. The minute you'd see a suspicious light you wouldn't take a chance; you'd just hit the jug and break it so if the Government men stopped you, they couldn't do anything because they didn't have any evidence.[254]

Darensbourg was probably not aware of the legacy of Williamson County's chief "Revenu-er" S. Glenn Young, hired by local business interests in 1924 to privately enforce Prohibition laws. The anonymous author of *The Life and Exploits of S. Glenn Young: World-Famous Law Enforcement Officer* believed the moral authorities of Williamson County "had come to the conclusion that through the enforcement of law, the foreigner within our gates must be forcibly taught that America is no place in which to perpetuate European evils, here placed under ban by law, that to enjoy American privileges America's laws must be respected."[255]

Young's apologist noted that all that was needed was "cohesion, unified action" to tame the nearby town of Colp, "another lawless community and the scene of frequent shootings…commonly known as Pistol City, a town more than half negro and foreign."[256] To Young's defender, Herrin was a "bootlegger's Mecca"; the city of Herrin was "by no means clean."[257] Young was hired to provide cohesion in the form of a private army of Ku Klux Klan members.

So zealous were Young's enforcers that if Joe Darensbourg and his buddies had made the mistake of shattering their liquor jugs atop a paved road, the "Revenu-ers would have a sponge in their pockets. There'd be some liquid left on the cement and they'd stick the sponge down there and squeeze into a jar they had. All they needed was a couple of teaspoonfuls and they'd arrest you."[258]

The *Belleville Daily Advocate* reported that Williamson County on January 11, 1924, was "a bit of hell while S. Glenn Young and his Ku Klux Klan legions were conducting extensive liquor raids." The paper also noted that "200 men armed with revolvers were ready to riot."[259]

Darensbourg may not have been aware of the 1900 Robert Charles race riots that left twenty-seven dead in New Orleans[260] or even the terrorizing 1910 Jack Johnson/Jim Jeffries boxing match race riots. He did know he was a mixed-race Catholic who could slip between the Black world and the white world easily. But what fate would have befallen him if he had been arrested by one of Young's Klan enforcers? Maybe he felt his Creole status would offer him some protection? At least he wasn't foreign.

Giovanni Picco, the Italian vice consul at Springfield, protested the harsh treatment suspects received when Young's forces descended on their homes and businesses. "The wives and children of the Italians were threatened with revolvers and the raiders used the vilest of language," Picco said. "They took money, rings and broke up furniture and other property. In one Italian home the raiders broke up a crucifix and a rosary."[261]

The French government made a similar protest and claimed the "dry raids [were] in fact pillages…and the raider made away with everything they could lay their hands upon, from baby rattles to valuable rings, money and heirlooms."[262]

It appears Doc Moon's Medicine Show wandered into Little Egypt in the summer of 1926 after the worst of S. Glenn Young's fascism (and his shootout death) but just in time for a gang war between Birger and his former allies, the Shelton brothers.

As Harrisburg and nearby Marion grew, so did the roadhouses. They had always been around, but the modern proliferation of automobiles, new roads and Prohibition made these "previously remote establishments readily accessible."[263] Many of them were sleazy joints, but some were full-fledged nightclubs that featured big-name bands and floor shows. But mainly they were a place to get illegal booze.

Charlie Birger's Shady Rest was probably a combination of the two. It was labeled by a contemporary of Birger as "the most notorious resort in the southern part of the state and attracted gamblers and others from far and near."[264] The first thing a motorist saw when approaching its location on State Highway 13 between Harrisburg and Marion was a small barbecue stand that sold soda pop (and under-the-table beer and whiskey). An enticing sign near the entrance advertised "Sixty Acres of Free Camping Ground," the woods offering a great place to hide a whiskey caravan of smuggled liquor from Florida.[265]

It's likely Doc Moon knew of Birger's operation in Little Egypt and moved the medicine show to Harrisburg, Birger's hometown, because he needed to replenish his alcohol stock. The musicians quickly learned of the Shady Rest and its band.

"The guys was talking about a terrific piano player and banjo player they had at the Shady Rest, a roadhouse about ten miles from Harrisburg, and naturally you could get liquor there," Darensbourg said.

Joe could not recollect the banjo/guitar player other than his name was Baker, and there was also a drummer named Jack Popper. But he remembered pianist Eddie Miller, known as the "Sheik of the Keyboard."[266] Miller recorded player piano rolls in Chicago for the piano manufacturers[267] and was featured regularly on Harrisburg's WEBQ radio station.[268]

Birger heard the jam session and offered Doc Moon's band a gig.

"We said yes," Joe said. "I said right there and then I didn't pay for this saxophone and told Charlie I owed ninety dollars. Charlie told the cashier to give me the money, just like that. I practically didn't play clarinet at all then, just alto saxophone, and it was a sax player that Charlie wanted."[269]

Doc Moon was upset and complained that Darensbourg didn't give him but three days' notice. That was unfortunate for Moon, but Birger biographer author Gary Deneal observed that Birger, who normally hired local Illinois bands, got "lucky once when a medicine show came through Harrisburg, boasting surefire cures for age-old ills and a band composed of silver strings."[270] Darensbourg probably teamed up with the popular local Black groups from Harrisburg's east end that included saxophonist Alvin Woods and drummer Charles Lennox.[271]

While in Harrisburg, Darensbourg was exposed to a musical technique that propelled his 1958 recording of "Yellow Dog Blues" onto the charts.[272]

Darensbourg was courting an attractive woman named Bessie who invited him to her house for dinner. To impress her with his musical skill, he brought his clarinet and saxophone. She countered that her little brother was a pretty good musician himself.

"Would you like to hear Harry play clarinet?" she asked. "He can do something on a clarinet not many people can do, although he's only twelve."

I said OK. I figured this little guy couldn't play a damn thing anyway. So, he picks up the clarinet, starts playing a tune, and he's doing the slap-tongue. I had heard slap-tonguing done before, but I never tried to do it. I was flabbergasted and fascinated by little Harry's playing. But I was kind of embarrassed too. Anyway, when he gets through playing this girl Bessie said "Joe, can you do that on a clarinet?" I says, "Oh, sure." She says, "Well, let's see you do it." So right away I had to make some kind of an excuse. I think I told her I had a toothache. Really, I felt like breaking the clarinet over this little dude's head. I wound up walking out of the house, mad, breaking up with the girl; and on top of that, I didn't get my dinner. But from then on, I vowed that I would learn how to do the slap-tongue, although up to that time I didn't know the technique of it. I tried and tried for a year and by trial and error it finally came to me, thank the Lord.[273]

"Slap-tongue is like spitting something off the end of your tongue while playing the reed," Darensbourg said. "You create a suction between the tongue and reed, so as to make the 'slap' sound."[274]

Despite the musical education, the Shady Rest was "no place for a preacher's son."[275] Customers came from far and wide to watch the "Blonde Bombshell" do her hoochie-koochie dance. (She wanted to do it nude, but that's where Charlie drew the line.)[276] They also came for prostitutes, a cockfighting arena, a dog-fighting pit and eagle and monkey cages.[277]

Monkeys?

When it came to people or animals, "Charlie went from one extreme to another," Darensbourg said. "He was kind-hearted in some ways, and he loved animals. He had pet bulldogs that would fight and fighting roosters, too, but his favorite was a little pet monkey named Jacko."[278]

The monkey, kept on a long chain so he could run up and down the trees, got Joe in trouble when he gave the pet some homebrew. Jacko soon began to feel the effects of the beer, but when one of the men threw a rubber snake near the macaque, poor Jacko had a fit. He tried to escape up the tree to get away from the perceived threat but was so drunk he made it only halfway up before falling down to the ground. Jacko again recognized the menacing shape of the snake and went into hysterics. The exhausted monkey passed out.

Birger drove up and saw how the musicians had abused his pet. "It took a couple of guys to keep him from killing us all," Darensbourg said. "He was on the verge of giving us a pistol-whipping. It was cruel what we did to poor little Jacko."[279]

Birger often displayed a tender heart. He brought coal and groceries to the widows of Harrisburg. And he loved his pets even though he made his beloved dogs fight to the death. But he so loved Jacko that he rushed the monkey to the hospital to see a doctor—not a veterinarian, a licensed MD. The docs got Jacko stabilized.

Darensbourg knew he was in the soup. One of Birger's men told him, "I'm telling you guys, you in trouble. You better stay here and take care of that monkey and pray that he lives. If he don't, you better go join your circus now."[280]

For good measure, Birger directed a murderous threat directly to Joe. "Goddam, how could you do this?" Birger said. "If that monkey dies, I better see none of you guys. I'm gonna kill every one of you."[281]

Darensbourg believed Charlie. Fortunately, Jacko recovered.

Birger had bigger problems than just dealing with an alcoholic monkey. He and the Sheltons, Carl, Earl and Bernie, allies during the Klan war and partners in a slot machine operation, began a feud in the summer of 1926 that developed into the kind of gang war seen in the movies. Darensbourg attributed the feud to a falling out over slot machine proceeds.[282]

Birger and the Sheltons began placing slot machines in Williamson County in December 1925, with Birger providing the capital and the Sheltons paying protection money to the local authorities. The first collector, identified only as "Johnson," took in the proceeds for $120 a week. The first take, hampered by the district attorney's temporary crackdown, was disappointing. Birger put in his man, John Howard, for $100 a week. Howard collected $1,700 in five weeks, but only $300 was remitted to the Sheltons. Then Birger fired Howard and replaced him with Ward "Casey" Jones. The fired Howard tattled and told Carl that Charlie had shorted him on the slots.[283]

Charlie was unaware of Howard's subterfuge when Earl Shelton requested a dogfight with Birger's kennel. Earl lied when he told Charlie his dog weighed sixty-three pounds; his fighter really was ten pounds heavier than Charlie's canine. Charlie, enraged that his dog had been unfairly outmatched, drew his weapon. Rudy Walker, "Boots" Dillard and "Pink" Whitehouse were eyewitnesses. Said Walker:

> *They had a shootout in the chicken arena. Me and Boots stood behind one of those big old-fashioned pot-bellied stoves and the bullets were going clink-clink as they hit the corrugated metal on the building, you know. "Boots," I said, "can you get out through that hole there?" That was where Birger had cut an oval place for his little puppy to get in for the night. He said, "I don't know." "Well," I said, "I'm going out through there, I can't get out through the door." Just one door to the place. And I got out there, so I pulled Boots through. He got hung in it and I pulled him through and took all the skin off his back. Well. Pink was still bigger than Boots, and he crawled on his hands and knees till he got around to the door, and he never got hit. Me and Boots beat him out of there. They was still shooting inside. I don't know how many was hit. I got out of there as quick as I could. I never will forget what Pink said when he got in his truck. "By golly, that ain't no place for a preacher's son, is it?"[284]*

Obviously, the Klan's Gestapo Prohibition enforcement tactics were bad for Birger and Shelton's business, but the Klan's reign seemed to be over after the April 1926 violence. But if the hotheaded bosses couldn't keep from shooting at each other, how could they expect their underlings not to act on old grudges against Klan "detectives," some of whom were still seen

Charlie Birger and his gang. Birger is sitting on the porch railing at the far right. Baton Rouge musician Joe Darensbourg, perhaps a bit thrilled by gangster Birger of Harrisburg, Illinois, left Doc Moon's Medicine Show in 1926 to perform at the Shady Rest roadhouse in the southern Illinois area known as Little Egypt. Unaware of the labor violence of the 1921 Herrin Massacre, the Ku Klux Klan enforcement of Prohibition laws and the bad blood between Birger and the Shelton gang, Darensbourg was shot in 1926 and left for dead in a gang war. Birger would later hang in 1928 for the murder of the West City mayor. *Library of Congress.*

around Williamson County sporting official badges, "the sacred emblem of the Klan"?[285] Alliances were shifting.

The upcoming gang war simmered in the summer of 1926, a fact recognized by the editor of the *Marion Evening Post* when he wrote, "This poor old news writer continues his advice and warns all who value life, liberty and pursuit of happiness, home and heaven to stay away from such places [Williamson County]."[286]

But violent activities intensified that summer. A gangster named Oklahoma Hardin was shot six times at Mildred's Place roadhouse, a Birger location, on July 12, 1926.[287] Shelton gang member Harry Walker was present.[288] Then Shelton gang members "Blackie" Armes, "Jardown" Armes and Harry Walker were arrested for assault in attacks on Klan informants.[289]

William Unsell, an elderly rural mail carrier, was robbed on August 5 by Joe Chesnas and two others. Chesnas, a young friend of Charlie Birger, shot and killed the old man three nights later because he was fearful of being identified.[290]

John Howard, a former Birger slot machine collector, was killed by a shotgun blast on August 16 as a result of a "gambling and drinking brawl, which had been in progress Sunday afternoon and night."[291]

Shelton gang member Harry Walker and Everett Smith were killed on August 22 in a roadhouse shooting north of Marion.[292] This may have been the incident in which Joe Darensbourg was shot and left for dead. How did he get involved? He blamed the piano player. Again, music played a fateful role in Joe's life.

"We had this nutty piano player that was telling people that he was part of Charlie's gang, until the word got out that the music was just a front and we was actually part of the gang," Darensbourg said. "One night we was coming back from another of Charlie's places where we'd been working and we stopped at another roadhouse at Marion, about ten miles from the Shady Rest. A white girl named Ruby, a fine entertainer round there, was singing, and we stopped off to hear her. This was when this song 'Go Back Where You Stayed Last Night' had just come out. Ruby moved around all the roadhouses singing."

Darensbourg got some of the details wrong in his *Jazz Odyssey*, and the *Murphysboro Daily Independent* provided few corroborations. Ruby was probably one of the "recently imported…singers of undisputed ability who have drawn trade from the other places," the *Independent* wrote in its August 24, 1926 edition.[293]

Even though Darensbourg was enjoying himself listening to Ruby, he was wary.

"The next thing you know the Shelton Gang was out, really looking for Charlie. Sometimes we'd ride with Charlie, and if he'd been with us, they'd have killed all of us," Darensbourg recollected. "So, when we stopped at the roadhouse, the Shelton guys was laying in wait for us. They actually didn't mean to kill us, just wanted to scare the hell out of us, which they did. First of all, they pistol whipped me and creased my skull with a bullet, shot me in the arm and leg and then left me for dead. They killed two of the other guys."[294]

Darensbourg's details are muddled. He identifies one of his assailants as "Blackie" Shelton and another as "Bill." In all likelihood, he was talking about Monroe "Blackie" Armes of the Shelton gang. Armes *was* arrested in the Walker murder.[295]

"I know who did most of the damage, a guy named Bill. I knew this guy and if it wasn't for [Blackie], he'd have killed me. He didn't like me on account of some gal he had that I was fooling around with," Darensbourg said.[296]

So how did Joe survive? Music lessons.

"Blackie used to fool around with the saxophone, and I'd show him a few things, so in a way I think he liked me," Darensbourg said. "It was him that said, 'Don't hit the guy no more or shoot him no more. I think he's already dead.'"[297]

After the attack, Darensbourg crawled to the car and drove himself to Birger's Harrisburg house.

"Charlie took me to the hospital and told the doctor, 'This man's been in an automobile accident,' and one of the doctors—I guess he didn't know Charlie—'No, this man's been shot,'" Darensbourg said. "So Charlie said, 'Listen, I'm Charlie Birger and I'm telling you this man has been in an automobile accident. OK?' After that the doctor put in a report that I was in an accident."[298]

It's curious why Birger wanted to cover up Darensbourg's gunshot wounds. The *Murphysboro Daily Independent Post* didn't have all the facts either. "Reports that two other men were injured, one from Marion, and taken to out-of-town hospital, lacks verification."[299]

Darensbourg didn't care. The glamor of encountering Al Capone, Machine Gun Jack McGurn, Bugsy Moran, the Egan Rats and the Purple Gang wasn't worth being laid up in the hospital for two weeks. He had time to think on his four-month stay in Little Egypt. "I was determined to get away from the Shady Rest," he said.[300]

"Charlie asked me, did I want to get even, because he was gonna set up a trap to kill some of them," Darensbourg said. "I just told Charlie, no. I wanted to get the hell away from there and forget all about it. Charlie did kill some of them afterwards."[301]

Darensbourg landed a job playing music in the Al G. Barnes circus. He said Birger came to the hospital, brought him a *Billboard* magazine to look for a band job and gave him a couple hundred dollars.[302]

"He was a pretty rough guy, but he was always good to musicians," Darensbourg said. "He was wonderful to me, and I never did pay him back for that saxophone."

Darensbourg left Harrisburg just before the real gang war got started, but he must have kept his eye out for news of Charlie Birger because he wrote about him in *Jazz Odyssey*.

Birger and the Sheltons were responsible for the building of armored vehicles to attack each other; the September 6 shooting of the state's attorney; the burning of the County Line roadhouse; assassinations of many gang members and their wives; the murder of the mayor of Colp; the attempted November 10 bombing of the Shady Rest with a homemade bomb tossed

Joe Darensbourg, wounded and left for dead in gangland violence, left Little Egypt by getting a gig with the Al G. Barnes Circus band. Darensbourg said *Billboard* magazine advertised pages of musician jobs for medicine shows, circuses, boat jobs, minstrel shows, stock company shows and roadhouses. In 1924, New Orleans clarinetist Willie Eli Humphrey (*second from left*) also performed with the Al G. Barnes Circus band. *New Orleans Jazz Museum.*

from a passing automobile; the November 12 bombing of the Shady Rest with a bomb dropped from an airplane; a bank robbery in Pocahontas, Illinois; the assassination of the mayor of West City (December 12); the total destruction of the Shady Rest (finally!) on January 8, 1927; the murder of a state trooper and his wife (January 17); and a second and third assassination attempt of the state's attorney on March 16 and August 7.[303]

Had Joe Darensbourg stuck around, he might have had the dubious honor of not only witnessing Ville Platte's first (and only) legal public hanging but also Illinois's penultimate hanging, the April 19, 1928 execution of Charlie Birger.[304] The Sheltons didn't fare much better. Carl's 1947 murder made the *New York Times*. Bernie was murdered in 1948. Earl survived several murder attempts and went straight. He moved to Florida and died an old man in 1986.[305]

Birger, like fellow serial murderer Euzebe Vidrine, made a statement from the gallows: "It's a beautiful world."[306]

Chapter 3

BORN ON THE FOURTH OF JULY

W as Louis Armstrong born on Independence Day? Absolutely. "Mayann told me that the night I was born there was a great big shooting scrape in the Alley and two guys killed each other. It was the Fourth of July, a big holiday in New Orleans, when almost anything can happen. Pretty near everybody celebrates with pistols, shot guns, or any other weapon that's handy," wrote Louis Armstrong in his 1954 autobiography, *Satchmo: My Life in New Orleans*.[307]

Armstrong was aware early on in his professional career of who he was and what he meant to Black America. He was also aware of what he meant to the entire American society by the time of his death in 1971. He was a prolific chronicler. In 1936, he published his first autobiography, *Swing That Music*. He was the first Black musician to do so. He was a faithful letter writer and wrote many other unpublished works in his den at his Queens, New York home. He also taped many of his performances and recorded conversations and his thoughts with visitors to his house.[308]

So how is it that August 4, 1901, is now the generally accepted birthdate of the great entertainer? Was Pops mistaken? Was he following the suit of "poor Black Americans [that], it was fashionable to adopt honorary birthdays," as one music blogger suggested?[309] Or was it a good showbiz date?[310]

In 1970, Armstrong, famous, wealthy and one of the most recognizable musicians in the world, made an appearance on the *Dick Cavett Show*. He performed one of his trademark songs, "I'll Be Glad When You're Dead, You Rascal, You."[311] It's fascinating that of all the hit songs Pops had ("Basin

Why did Louis Armstrong insist his birthday was July 4? A typical line in Armstrong bios goes something like this: "It was custom for poor blacks to adopt an honorary date as their birthday—often Christmas, or New Year's Day, or the Fourth of July." Such statements fail to grasp what Independence Day meant to the new citizens created by the United States' Fourteenth Amendment to the Constitution and their descendants. Armstrong may have insisted on celebrating his birthday on July 4 because Independence Day meant something significant to him about being an American. *Courtesy of the Louis Armstrong House Museum.*

Street Blues," "Blueberry Hill," "West End Blues," "Hello, Dolly"), the song he chose to perform on national television was a comic song about infidelity and murder. What was he really saying with that song? I'll be glad when this system of racism and discrimination is dead? If the youth of America was writing antiwar songs with transparent messages—"War" by Edwin Starr and the "I Feel Like I'm Fixin' to Die Rag" by Country Joe and the Fish[312] come to mind—why couldn't the elder statesman of jazz and pop music send a message too? The millions in the liberal Cavett audience were the perfect audience for the beloved Louis Armstrong. They got the joke, but did they miss the hidden transcript of "I'll Be Glad When You're Dead, You Rascal, You?" As assassinations, Vietnam and civil rights riots were in America's living rooms on a nightly basis, America enjoyed and needed the performances of the ostensibly happy-go-lucky Louis Armstrong. Louis couldn't mean anything sinister in a funny song like that, could he? But the message Louis was transmitting was loud and clear. His Fourth of July birthday was the first subject.

Cavett brought up the subject of Louis's birthday:

> **Dick Cavett**: *When were you born?*
> **Louis Armstrong**: *Nineteen hundred. Twelve o'clock at night.*
> **Dick Cavett**: *It is—it's twelve at night?*
> **Louis Armstrong**: *Yeah, they called me a—*
> **Dick Cavett**: *So how did they know whether your birthday was on the—what—your birthday's on the—I thought it was on the Fourth.*
> **Louis Armstrong**: *Well, I'm—no, I didn't ask Mama all that, I'm just glad to be here, I mean—I wouldn't interfere in her business, you know?*
> **Dick Cavett**: *No, no, I wouldn't—we—we have to take a message, we'll be right back.*[313]

There, Pops said it on national TV—he was born on the Fourth of July 1900, at twelve o'clock at night, never mind the quibble if it was July 4 at midnight, one minute before the next day.

Louis was coy about his birth year. On *Cavett*, he said it was 1900, and the talk-show host didn't bring up the subject again after the TV commercial. The date of Armstrong's birth might have never come back up if weren't for researchers pointing out discrepancies in Pops's permanent record. The first time Louis himself ever wrote down his birthdate on an official form was for the United States military draft World War I registration. Possibly to appear older, he marked July 4, 1900, as his date of birth. However, decades later, he recorded a DOB of July 4, 1901, on his Social Security application in 1937 when he was filming *Every Day's a Holiday* at Paramount Studios.[314]

In 1981, more evidence to support a July 4, 1901 birthdate was uncovered by Alan Kimble and his wife, Sylvia Kimble Washington (the granddaughter of Captain Joseph Jones, the disciplinarian who operated the Colored Waif's Home). The Kimbles found records from the Waif's Home in her grandfather's house that showed Louis Armstrong had been sent to the Waif's Home in 1910 for a general rousting of juvenile undesirables.[315] The Waif's Home records indicated Louis was nine years old the first time he was sent to the detention home. The October 22, 1910 *Picayune* published the police report:

Quite a number of boys were arrested yesterday for being dangerous and suspicious characters, no less than eight being brought to the Juvenile court.

Round Up—Clarence Roberts, of No. 941 St. Mary Street, and John Centilivere, of St. Ferdinand and Chartres Streets, were arrested at Common and St. Charles Streets by Patrolman Mike Sanmovich while Detectives Charles Mellen, William Kennedy, John Dantonio and Patrolman Anthony Sabrier arrested Henry Smith, of Lafayette and Fulton; James Kent, of 338 Saratoga Street; Archie Anderson, of 631 Dryades Street; Willie Telfry, of 416 S. Franklin Street; Louis Armstrong, of Perdido, between Liberty and Franklin streets; and Eddie Moore, of Liberty, between Gravier and Perdido streets.[316]

Three years later, the *Times-Democrat* reported the arrest that sent Armstrong to the Waif's Home. The clip mentioned Armstrong's prior arrest and, ultimately, yielded another clue to his birth year:

Few Juveniles Arrested
Very few arrests of minors were made Tuesday, and the bookings in the Juvenile Court are not more than the average. Six white boys were arrested in Canal street for disturbing the peace, and one for being drunk. The most serious case was that of Louis Armstrong, a twelve-year old negro, who discharged a revolver at Rampart and Perdido streets. Being an old offender he was sent to the negro [sic] Waif's home. The other boys were paroled.[317]

"An old offender" was the clue. Alan Kimble, who had protected the records from the Waif's Home since 1980 through a lost job, depression and divorce, finally got *Times-Picayune* writer James Karst interested in the Waif's Home records. Karst uncovered Armstrong's previous arrest, and another small piece of the trumpet player's life fell into place. The first arrest and Waif's Home stay of nine-year-old Louis solidified 1901 as his birth year. Armstrong historian Ricky Riccardi termed the discovery of the earlier arrest as "incredible."[318]

Whether Pops was born on July 4, 1900 (as he sometimes claimed), or July 4, 1901 (as he also sometimes claimed), was all rendered moot in 1988, when researcher Tad Jones, a well-known New Orleans writer and researcher, found Louis Armstrong's baptismal record at Sacred Heart Catholic Church, 130 South Lopez Street.[319] Louis Armstrong's birthday was August 4, 1901, the record showed. The proof was in black-and-white.

Jones said he felt "surprised" at finding the baptismal record hiding in plain sight, "but only because it had been sitting there for 87 years and no one else had found it. It wasn't like looking into King Tut's tomb."[320]

The *Times-Picayune* publicized Jones's discovery in the September 24, 1988 "Armstrong: Give or Take a Year" story by reporter Bruce Eggler. A photo of the Sacred Heart baptismal record book was included. Then, on the next Fourth of July edition, the *Picayune* ran the follow-up "Happy Unbirthday, Satchmo," with an explanation of why Mayann and Pops might have chosen July 4 as the date of her son's birth.

"For a poor and ill-educated black man not to know his birthday was common in those days, and scholars figured that Armstrong simply borrowed the nation's birthday for his own. He apparently had no birthday celebrations as a child," wrote Eggler.[321]

Lawrence Bergreen followed suit in *Louis Armstrong: An Extravagant Life*. "It was custom for poor blacks to adopt an honorary date as their birthday—often Christmas, or New Year's Day, or the Fourth of July," he wrote.[322]

Such statements fail to grasp what Independence Day meant to the new citizens created by the United States' Fourteenth Amendment to the constitution. Mayann, one generation removed from slavery, might have had a deeper appreciation of the national holiday as well. From 1776, when the Declaration of Independence was written, to 1868, with the passage of the Fourteenth Amendment, the promise of that famous document only applied to white society.

Black abolitionist Frederick Douglass first delivered his "What, to the Slave, Is the Fourth of July?" speech in 1852:

> *What, to the American slave, is your 4th of July? I answer; a day that reveals to him, more than all other days in the year, the gross injustice and cruelty to which he is the constant victim. To him, your celebration is a sham; your boasted liberty, an unholy license; your national greatness, swelling vanity; your sounds of rejoicing are empty and heartless; your denunciation of tyrants, brass fronted impudence; your shouts of liberty and equality, hollow mockery; your prayers and hymns, your sermons and thanksgivings, with all your religious parade and solemnity, are, to Him, mere bombast, fraud, deception, impiety, and hypocrisy—a thin veil to cover up crimes which would disgrace a nation of savages. There is not a nation on the earth guilty of practices more shocking and bloody than are the people of the United States, at this very hour.*[323]

Given the lapse of time from when Douglass first delivered his famous speech, it is understandable that late twentieth-century writers (and most folks, white and Black)[324] might have been unaware of the deeper significance Independence Day took on for the post–Civil War emancipated slave.

On July 9, 1868, with the ratification of the Fourteenth Amendment, nearly four million freedmen were finally admitted to the Union. To these newly minted American citizens, the Fourth of July now meant they were officially part of the United States of America and "endowed by their Creator with certain unalienable Rights, that among these are Life, Liberty and the pursuit of Happiness."[325]

Ten years after the Civil War, Douglass updated his speech and wondered what America had in store for Black people. "If war among the whites brought peace and liberty to the blacks," he said, "what will peace among the whites bring?"[326]

Pursuing happiness was not fair. According to Randy Newman's ironic 1974 anthem "Rednecks," peace among the whites brought the Black man freedom to be "put in cages not only in the South but in Harlem in New York City, the South Side and West Side of Chicago, Hough in Cleveland, East St. Louis, Fillmore in San Francisco, Roxbury in Boston."[327]

By the time Louis Armstrong was ten years old, he had witnessed the race riots caused by the Jack Johnson/Jim Jeffries heavyweight fight, streetcar segregation and the "freedom" to be put in the Waif's Home.[328] And when it came time to register for the army draft, he chose the Fourth of July as his birthday. Bergreen suggested Louis chose the date because he had a "pride in a country and a region" even though that country and region "wanted nothing to do with his kind."[329]

Louis was certainly proud of New Orleans, but the feeling for his country must have had a different meaning for him and his parents than it did for white city residents. Did he fully comprehend what his citizenship in the United States meant or what it had cost? What thoughts might have entered his mind when he first wrote down July 4, 1900, as his date of birth for the New Orleans draft board, a government entity? Was he empowered? For sure he knew he had very little power as a poorly educated Black man. Did he know that there was a history of white disdain for the federal government's Fourth of July holiday in the South? Historian Joe Gray Taylor said, "Independence Day, which had been a holiday of all before the war, became a freedman's holiday during Reconstruction. Whites might not work on the Fourth of July, but it was Blacks who held parades, picnics, and dances."[330]

Was Armstrong or his mother familiar with Frederick Douglass's "What, to the Slave, Is the Fourth of July?"[331] Was the "mysterious spiritual telegraph which runs through the slave population" still operating among the descendants of the freedmen and communicating with the residents of Jane Alley, Uptown, the District and Tremé? Was the message, "You are bona fide, and the Fourth of July is your day to celebrate your citizenship"?

Prior to the Civil War, white Americans celebrated Independence Day with "feasts, parades, and copious quantities of alcohol."[332] It was "almost the only holy-day kept in America."[333] But the Confederacy's defeat created economic and social hardship, and the day itself reminded many southerners of bitter military defeat. The Mississippi River town of Vicksburg fell to Grant's army on July 4, 1863. Though not as geographically close, the decisive Battle of Gettysburg was ended on July 3 of the same year. In general, July 4 was not a welcome holiday.[334]

An ambivalent tone and downright hostility toward the national holiday were reflected in the Louisiana newspapers from 1866 all the way up to 1898, when Spanish-American War fever once again made nationalism fashionable.

In the seat of state government, the July 5, 1867 Baton Rouge *Tri-Weekly Advocate* solemnly announced, "The Fourth passed quietly away. There was a meeting of colored people under the market, but no cannon were fired, no processions organized. At night some rockets went up, a few dozen Roman candles lit up the streets, the rain set in and the Fourth of July passed away."[335] The *New Orleans Daily Picayune* July 3, 1872 edition merely labeled the nation's birthday as a "political holiday."[336]

As the reunited nation moved closer to the centennial anniversary of the Declaration of Independence and the birth of the United States, the media remained lukewarm to the federal holiday. The 1874 *Picayune* edition noted the day would not be like past Fourths:

Not after the manner of our ancestors will we celebrate to-day. There will be no blowing of trumpets, no rattling of drums, no fizzling of fire crackers; our bold militia have postponed their martial parade. There will be no firing of cannon; and, lastly, not a speech; no unfledged orator soaring heedlessly through the air on the American eagle.[337]

The 1875 July 4 edition declared the Fourth as the "Day We Do Not Celebrate"[338] and scoffed at the celebrations of the Black community. "Of latter years it has been the habit of the colored militia and the metropolitan police to straggle tamely through the streets, exciting no ardor by the way and reaping scant reward save perspiration and fatigue."[339] The *Picayune* warmed up a bit in the centennial year and described a Fourth of July parade as a "brilliant procession"[340] and "the streets and the shipping at the Levee were gay with flags and brilliant bunting,"[341] reflecting a reconciliation with the new status quo, but returned to its sardonic form the very next year when it sniped, "The day was not heralded in by the announcement of any brilliant display nor was there in point of fact, any extensive organized demonstration in honor of the anniversary celebration of the great event which moulded the destinies of this free land."[342]

Before the Civil War, American Blacks did not observe the Fourth of July because, as Frederick Douglass noted, "it is the birthday of *your* [italics mine] National Independence, and of *your* political freedom."[343] It is "a day that reveals to him [the slave], more than all other days in the year, the gross injustice and cruelty to which he is the constant victim....I am not included within the pale of this glorious anniversary!...This Fourth [of] July is yours not mine."[344] Douglass's speech was perhaps America's original uncomfortable truth.

Even though enslaved Blacks were often given July 4 off, with some believing the day to be Easter, Whitsuntide or midsummer,[345] free Blacks instead chose to observe July 5 "to better accentuate the difference between the high promises of the Fourth and the low realities of life for African Americans, while also avoiding confrontations with drunken white revelers."[346]

But emancipation and the Thirteenth, Fourteenth and Fifteenth Amendments gave citizenship rights to slaves, freed people of color and the Creole descendants of freed people of color. Southern Blacks could now share ownership of Independence Day with the majority-white population, and heartily celebrate they did, at least while under the protection of Reconstruction. They celebrated with fireworks and libations and gathered in public arenas to hear orators recite the Emancipation Proclamation, the Declaration of Independence and the Thirteenth Amendment, which abolished slavery.[347]

The Fourth of July was enthusiastically celebrated in Charleston, South Carolina, the state where the first shots of the Civil War were fired. From the late 1860s through the 1870s, Charleston's public Fourth of July celebration was truly a Black holiday.[348] The city's parade traveled down Meeting Street and ended at White Point Garden with speeches by the Black Republican leaders and eating, drinking, frolicking and dancing the too-la-loo.[349]

The white population "shut themselves within doors"[350] and tried to ignore the Black jubilee. It was a "a dreadful day," said one Charleston planter in a letter to his daughter.[351] A local merchant's journal observed that the federal holiday had become "a n----r day": "N----r procession, n----r dinner and balls and promenades" and "scarcely a white person seen in the streets."[352]

The Black observance continued even after federal troops were pulled out in some Louisiana cities. One such celebration involved a steamboat excursion organized in New Orleans to rendezvous with a large Black contingent on the grounds of the state capitol in Baton Rouge. The Black-owned July 12, 1879 *Weekly Louisianian* reported:

> *A line of procession was then formed and the Commandery as the guests o'*
> *the Masons of Baton Rouge, paraded through the principal streets with the*
> *Excelsior Band uniformed at its head. All along the line of march the streets*
> *were crowded with enthusiastic people, the marching and maneuvering of*
> *the Sir Knights drew forth hearty applause, the showing of the Commandery*
> *was beyond a doubt agreeably surprising to its friends in Baton Rouge.*
>
> *After the parade the Sir Knights with a few visiting friends were right*
> *royally entertained at a banquet given in their honor by the Stone Square*
> *Lodge at Liberty Hall. The moonlight pic-nic given for the benefit of the*
> *Commandery was a very joyous affair. The State House grounds were*
> *beautifully and brilliantly illuminated, beneath flowery bowers, handsomely*
> *decorated tables fairly groaning under the weight of cooling ices, wines and*
> *sweet meats in abundance.*[353]

The *Picayune* did notice Black celebrations, however. It noted in 1882, "The members of the ex–United States Colored Soldier and Sailor's Union celebrated the Fourth of July at Jackson Hall, corner of Franklin and Jackson streets, on Tuesday evening. Addresses were delivered by Col. James Lewis and Lawrence D. Hubbard, after which the remainder of the evening was occupied in dancing."[354]

Sentiments about the Fourth of July were not uniform across the state. The *Bossier Banner* couldn't bring itself to once mention the 1876 Centennial Fourth of July,[355] while New Iberia, the heart of Louisiana's sugar cane country where a large workforce was needed, seemed to be progressive and shared a parade with the freedmen. A crowd of ten thousand came out to celebrate. The *Louisiana Sugar Bowl* reported, "It was the first celebration in the history of our country, in which our white and colored citizens mutually participated and fraternized....To set aside race, color and the issues of the day, in a population so diverse and antagonistic as ours, was a success worthy of the Centennial hour."[356]

The paper observed the white part of the parade was a mile long, but the Black section was even longer, and despite the integrated celebration, the day was unmarred by "incidents or disorders of any sort."[357]

When tension between Spain and the United States erupted into the 1898 Spanish-American War, it sent a signal to whites that it was once again safe to celebrate their freedom from King George the tyrant. The *Picayune* reported it was time for "one of the greatest celebrations of the sort the United States has ever witnessed."[358] Admiral William Sampson certainly gave Americans something to hoot and holler about with the July 3 news of his "crushing blow to the Spanish fleet."[359] The *Picayune* devoted its entire front page to war news, but nearly all of page seven was filled with "for the first time since the civil war" stories of celebrations that even included Atlanta and Vicksburg, the site of the Confederacy's bitterest defeats.

By the year of Louis Armstrong's birth, 1901, white New Orleans had fully re-embraced Independence Day. A seven-column front-page headline proclaimed, "A GREAT FOURTH IN NEW ORLEANS"[360] and reported, "City park was the scene of a glorious Fourth. It was a grand, patriotic festival, planned and executed on a different order from the usual Fourth of July celebrations."[361] Racism and demeaning attitudes still prevailed in the newspaper, however, as it reported that one of the most popular attractions at the party was "throwing the eggs at the n----r's head."[362] For five cents, customers could throw rotten eggs at a Black person. It was laughed off as the foolish antics of the "customary side show class."[363]

Mayann Armstrong might have laughed at the hapless Black fool who taunted white folks into throwing rotten eggs at him, but it's highly likely she was aware of what the Fourth of July meant to her and her parents, born slaves.

But there was another epochal event in Louis Armstrong's life that might have made him acutely aware of the power of July 4. That was the day Black America celebrated the victory of heavyweight boxer Jack Johnson over Jim Jeffries, the "Great White Hope." Certainly, young Louis was aware of Jack Johnson. When Johnson defeated Jeffries in 1910, Louis was nine years old. He had rudimentary education and "could read the newspapers to the older folk in my neighborhood who helped mama to raise me."[364] Surely, precocious Louis, already selling newspapers, was aware of the sporting life. Armstrong reported in *My Life in New Orleans* that he was already "shooting dice for pennies or playing a little coon or blackjack."[365]

The Daily Picayune.

VOL. LXII.   NEW ORLEANS, MONDAY, JULY 4, 1898.   NO. 161.

A GLORIOUS FOURTH OF JULY.

Good News for America from Both the East and West Indies.

Admiral Sampson Has Destroyed All of Cervera's Ships But One.

General Shafter Has Demanded the Surrender of Santiago City,

And Will Probably Raise Old Glory Over the Place To-Day.

The First Expedition Arrived at Manila on Thursday Last.

Americans Raised Our Flag Over the Largest of the Group of Ladrone Islands.

(Special Dispatch to the Picayune and New York Herald, Copyright, 1898, by James Gordon Bennett.)

WASHINGTON, JULY 3.—President McKinley and his cabinet have been deliberating to-day upon important and gratifying news from the front. According to dispatches received from Colonel Allen, in charge of the cable station at Playa del Este, by General Greely, stationed in New York, and transmitted to the secretary of war, Admiral Sampson has met and destroyed all of Admiral Cervera's fleet except one vessel, which vessels of his squadron are now pursuing, and General Shafter has demanded and momentarily expects the surrender of Santiago. According to the message, which first came through the source indicated, Admiral Cervera's fleet, in desperate straits, made an effort to leave the harbor and run the gauntlet of the American fleet. He was partially successful, but was met by a fierce fire from the vessels of Admiral Sampson's squadron, which, following in hot pursuit, engaged and destroyed all the vessels of the Spanish squadron except one.

A later report was to the effect that Admiral Sampson had forced his way into the harbor and had destroyed all of Admiral Cervera's fleet, except one.

They have one dispatch from General Shafter, filed at 3 o'clock this afternoon. The general states that he has demanded and expects the surrender of Santiago. He also confirms the report, via Madrid to-night, to the effect that General Linares has been mortally wounded and that half of his command has been rendered hors du combat.

The President and his advisers are eagerly awaiting official dispatches from General Shafter or Admiral Sampson to know exactly what has happened. They feel satisfied that Admiral Sampson has met Cervera's fleet, and credit the report from Colonel Allen that they have all been destroyed except one, but they do not know whether the engagement occurred inside or outside of the harbor.

This statement was given out at the war department about midnight.

"PLAYA DEL ESTE, July 3.—General Shafter telegraphs early this morning: I sent a demand for the immediate surrender of Santiago, threatening to bombard the city. I believe the place will be surrendered."

This contradicts the report that General Shafter has fallen back.

The following dispatch was received at the war department:

"PLAYA DEL ESTE, July 3.—Siboney office confirms statement that all the Spanish fleet, except one warship, destroyed and burning on the beach. It was witnessed by Captain Smith, who told operator. No doubt of its correctness. ALLEN."

Another dispatch was received at the war department this afternoon from Colonel Wagner, stating that Pando had not yet arrived, and that his force consisted of only five thousand men.

General Garcia has occupied such a position with three thousand men as to prevent the entrance of Pando into Santiago.

From all the information the authorities have at hand, the authorities, at the hour this dispatch is filed, consider that Spain's naval power in the Atlantic has been destroyed and that Santiago de Cuba is now at the mercy of General Shafter's army and Admiral Sampson' fleet.

There was a conference at the white house between President McKinley, Vice President Hobart, Secretary Wilson, Postmaster General Smith, Secretary Alger, General Corbin, Assistant Secretary Alger. When it adjourned Secretary Alger stated that Mr. Allen was preparing a statement, which would be given out a few minutes later, as soon as the clerk could prepare and copy it.

Secretary Alger authorized this statement to-night:

"In answer to a dispatch sent by Secretary Alger to Major General Shafter, asking why he had not sent the government more dispatches, this cablegram was received:

"PLAYA DEL ESTE, Headquarters Fifth Army Corps, July 3.—Did not telegraph, as I was too busy looking after things that had to be attended to at once, and did not wish to send any news that was not fully confirmed.

"Spanish fleet left the harbor this morning and is reported as practically destroyed.

"I demanded the surrender of the city at 10 a. m. to-day. At this hour, 4:30 p. m., no reply has been received. Perfect quiet along the line.

"Situation has been precarious on account of difficulties of supplying command with food and tremendous fighting capabilities shown by the enemy from his almost impregnable position. SHAFTER."

This dispatch was received from Colonel Allen about 12:30 this morning:

"All the Spanish ships destroyed but one, and they are close after her. The Spaniards ran their ships close to shore, set them on fire and they exploded."

In answer to a cable sent Colonel Allen after the receipt of the first report concerning the destruction of Admiral Cervera's fleet, this cable was received by the president at 1 o'clock this morning:

"Report of destruction of Admiral Cervera's fleet confirmed. ALLEN."

A rumor is in circulation that Admiral Cervera is among the dead on the Spanish fleet. One report says he committed suicide. It may have been, however, that he remained on his flagship and perished when its magazines exploded.

(Special Cable to the Picayune and New York Herald, Copyright, 1898, by James Gordon Bennett.)

Hong Kong, via Paris, July 4.---The cruiser Charleston and transports arrived at Manila on June 30. Captured Guahan, largest of the Ladrones, on June 20.

After the Confederacy's Civil War defeat, Independence Day for southerners became the "day we do not celebrate," but it was a freedmen's holiday during Reconstruction. Whites might not work on the Fourth of July, but it was Blacks who held parades, picnics and dances. Nationalist fervor over 1898's Spanish-American War signaled to white southerners that it was ok to celebrate the United States again. *From the* Times-Picayune, *New Orleans.*

On July 4, 1910, when Louis Armstrong was nine years old, Black heavyweight boxing champion Jack Johnson defeated Jim Jeffries, the "Great White Hope." Race riots occurred in New Orleans and throughout the country (two were killed in Louisiana). Armstrong knew the Fourth of July, a powerful day for Black people, was a sensitive subject to white southerners, and that may have played a role in why he chose the date to celebrate his birthday. *Courtesy of the Louis Armstrong House Museum.*

In 1910, in the days leading up to the Jeffries fight, scarcely a day went by without a mention of the Black champion in the *Daily Picayune*. White New Orleans was obviously obsessed with Johnson, and there were more than two hundred stories mentioning him that year. And why not? Newspapers had discovered sensation sells, and no one created more of a visceral response than Jack Johnson.

Ever since Johnson won the heavyweight title from Tommy Burns in 1908, *Picayune* sportswriter Harry "Mack" McEnerny's weekly column, "Mack's Melange," had mentioned Johnson in nearly every edition.[366] White America could not wait for Jim Jeffries to reclaim the boxing title that was thought to be "the most prized possessions in the trophy room of white supremacy."[367]

Probably the thing that infuriated white boxing fans the most was Johnson's taunting verbal banter with his opponent and his ever-present smile. The "carefree negro smiled and smiled…and that is the story of the fight," wrote journalist Jack London, on hand to cover the Reno, Nevada fight for the *New York Herald* syndicate. His round-by-round account of the match was printed on the front page of the *Picayune*.

"Once again has Johnson sent down to defeat the chosen representative of the white race, and this time the greatest of them. And, as of old, it was play for Johnson."[368] London was not short of praise for the Black boxer. He described him as "the cool-headed negro," "cool as ice," who fought with "Chesterfieldian grace" and ultimately was an "amazing fighting mechanism."[369]

The fight today, and again I repeat, was great only in its significance. In itself, it was not great….Johnson played as usual with his opponent, not strong in the attack. Johnson, blocking and defending in masterly fashion, could afford to play. And he played and fought a white man, in the white man's audience. And the audience was a Jeffries audience.[370]

Louis remembered the day and the wave of violence afterward clearly:

> *I was scared, more scared than I was the day Jack Johnson knocked out Jim Jeffries. That day I was going to get my supply of papers from Charlie, who employed a good many colored boys like myself. On Canal Street I saw a crowd of colored boys running like mad toward me.*
>
> *I asked one of them what had happened.*
>
> *"You better get started, black boy," he said breathlessly as he started to pull me along. "Jack Johnson has just knocked out Jim Jeffries. The white boys are sore about it and they're going to take it out on us."*
>
> *He did not have to do any urging. I lit out and passed the other boys in a flash. I was a fast runner, and when the other boys reached our neighborhood, I was at home looking calmly out the window. The next day the excitement had blown over.*[371]

Louis downplayed the "excitement" and how it related to him, but race riots ensued across the country. Two in Louisiana were killed and three injured.[372] There were riots in nearly every major city in the country.[373] Fourth of July exuberance, alcohol and the thrill of Johnson's victory obviously affected people's better judgment. Nelson Turner of New York was nearly lynched when he yelled to a crowd of white men, "We blacks put one over on you whites, and we are going to do more to you."[374]

Jack Johnson remained in the news throughout his heavyweight career and undoubtedly was a topic of conversation on the streets, bars and tonks throughout Armstrong's Battlefield neighborhood and the Storyville District. What did the victory mean to Black people? Harlem Renaissance poet/musician/composer William Waring Cuney wrote "My Lord, What a Morning" years after the fight:

> *Oh, my Lord*
> *What a morning,*
> *Oh, my Lord,*
> *What a feeling,*
> *When Jack Johnson*
> *Turned Jim Jeffries'*
> *Snow-white face*
> *Up to the ceiling.*[375]

New Orleans newspaper coverage of Johnson continued for years, and Louis never forgot Jack Johnson's Fourth of July victory over the white boxer. Did it help fuel his competitive fire? By the time Louis wrote his birthdate down, probably for the first time ever, on his 1918 draft registration,[376] he had witnessed and participated in many cutting contests on the streets of New Orleans. Outside of the Crescent City, he displayed an "angry intensity"[377] during these exhibitions that "shocked" musicians outside New Orleans. Musicologist Thomas Brothers mentioned the embarrassment of the excellent trumpeter Jabbo Smith in a 1920s New York cutting contest and the total destruction of challenger Johnny Dunn of Memphis. So thorough was Pops's victory that poor Johnny didn't even stick around to hear the crowd's final approval of the young man with a horn from New Orleans.[378]

There is other evidence that Armstrong was aware of the things that needled white folks. As he was performing as a teenager in New Orleans, he knew all the popular songs of the day. Though Bolden was long gone from the music scene when Armstrong began performing, given Armstrong's wit and keen sense of his social standing, he must have heard and laughed at versions of Bolden's "Funky Butt" hit with the "Mr. Lincoln" lyrics. New Orleans jazz chronicler Danny Barker said the lyrics included lines that obviously annoyed white folks:

> *I thought I heer'd Mr. Lincoln say,*
> *Rebels close them plantations and let all them n-----s out.*
> *You gonna lose this war, git on your knees and pray,*
> *That's the words I heer'd Mr. Lincoln say.*[379]

Even as a child, Armstrong was fully aware of the hatred the old Confederate veterans had for Blacks:

> *At ten years old I could see—the Bluffings that those Old Fat Belly Stinking very Smelly Dirty White Folk were putting Down. It seemed as though the only thing they cared about was their Shot Guns or those Old time Shot Guns which they had strapped around them. So they get full of their Mint Julep or that bad whiskey, the poor white Trash were Guzzling down, like water, then when they get so Damn Drunk until they'd go out of their minds—then it's N----r Hunting time. Any N----r. They wouldn't give up until they would find one. From then on, Lord have mercy on the poor Darkie. Then they would Torture the poor Darkie, as innocent as he may*

be. They would get their usual Ignorant Chess Cat laughs before they would shoot him down—like a Dog. My my my, those were the day.[380]

Did he know that the Fourth of July was a "Black" holiday? It seems obvious. He knew it was the day when Jack Johnson "turned Jim Jeffries' snow-white face up to the ceiling." He knew white southerners were sensitive about their defeat in the Civil War. Was writing down "July 4, 1900" on the government's draft card an act of defiance that went unnoticed by his biographers?

Throughout his life, Louis understood the prejudice Black America faced. He recognized (and participated in) the small protests Black New Orleanians engaged in on the segregated streetcars:

There is something funny about those [FOR COLORED PASSENGERS ONLY] *signs on the street cars in New Orleans. We colored folks used to get real kicks out of them when we got on a car at the picnic grounds or at Canal Street on a Sunday evening when we outnumbered the white folks. Automatically we took the whole car over, sitting as far up front as we wanted to. It felt good to sit up there once in a while. We felt a little more important than usual. I can't explain why exactly, but maybe it was because we weren't supposed to be up there.*[381]

By 1929, Armstrong had become more than just a jazz musician. At that point, biographer Ricky Riccardi believed him a "masterful pop artist…at almost all times in his career [and]…more popular with the general public than simply with jazz fans."[382] He could be hammy, and his "blinding smile and eye-rolling stage persona"[383] as well as his lofty position attracted cries of "Uncle Tom," a criticism that Louis was aware of.[384]

He was also aware of his good fortune but equally concerned about social justice. When Arkansas governor Orval Faubus tried to prevent nine Black schoolchildren from integrating Little Rock Central High School in 1957, Pops said, "I've had a beautiful life over forty years in music, but I feel the downtrodden situation the same as any other Negro. My parents and family suffered through all of that old South and things are new now."[385]

At the time, Louis was asked to represent America overseas as a goodwill ambassador to show the Cold War world the promise of democracy, but he criticized President Dwight Eisenhower, who was slow to federally intervene in Little Rock. Satchmo was performing in Grand Forks, North Dakota, when Larry Lubenow, a young reporter for the *Grand Forks Herald*, conned

'Government Can Go To Hell'

'Satchmo' Swings Into Ike, Cancels Trip To Russia

GRAND FORKS, N.D. (P) — Trumpet player Louis (Satchmo) Armstrong said yesterday he's given up plans for a government-sponsored trip to Russia because, "The way they are treating my people in the South, the government can go to hell."

Here for a concert, Armstrong said President Eisenhower had "no guts" and described Arkansas Gov. Orval Faubus as an "uneducated plow boy."

'JUST FINE'

Armstrong reaffirmed the statements he made to a Grand Forks Herald reporter. Shown a copy of the story that had been written on the basis of his remarks, Armstrong said "That's just fine. Don't take nothing out of that story. That's just what I said and still say."

He wrote the word "solid" at the bottom of the account and affixed his signature.

It said the President is "two-faced" and has allowed Faubus to run the federal government.

At the Newport, R.I., vacation White House, Presidential Press Secretary James C. Hagerty declined comment.

"It's getting almost so bad a

LOUIS ARMSTRONG
. . . 'solid.'

colored man hasn't got any country," the Negro entertainer said.

"Don't get me wrong," he added, "the South is full of intelligent white people, it's bad the lower class people who make all the noise, though."

'PUBLICITY STUNT'

Armstrong said that use of National Guard troops to prevent school integration at Little Rock was "a publicity stunt led by the greatest of all publicity hounds." He said such things have a bad effect on relations with other countries.

"The people over there ask me what's wrong with my country, what am I supposed to say?"

He said if he ever does go through with his proposed trip to Russia, "I'll do it on my own."

In Washington, the State Department declined to comment on Armstrong's statements. Officials made no attempt, however, to hide the concern they caused.

Armstrong was regarded by the State Department as perhaps the most effective unofficial good will ambassador this country has.

Louis Armstrong was very concerned about civil rights and disgusted with President Eisenhower's lack of action during the Little Rock school integration crisis of 1957. Armstrong was aware of his role as goodwill ambassador on jazz tours to foreign countries the United States courted as allies during the Cold War, but he threatened to quit if changes weren't made. *From the* Tampa Bay Times, *Florida.*

his way into Pops's hotel room and an interview. Pops, dressed in a Hawaiian shirt and Bermuda shorts, warmed up to the kid as he ate his lobster dinner.[386]

"He just exploded," Lubenow said, when he informed Armstrong that Grand Forks was the hometown of U.S. District Court judge Ronald Davies, whose ruling in support of integration led to the Little Rock crisis.[387] The *Grand Forks Herald* didn't take the story, so Lubenow filed it with the Associated

Press. Newspapers from Richmond to Biloxi to Great Falls, Montana, let the world know that Armstrong had given up a government-sponsored trip to Russia because of "the way they are treating my people in the South, the government can go to hell."[388]

Along with a few choice expletives,[389] Armstrong said Eisenhower was "two-faced" and had "no guts."[390] He said the president had "allowed Faubus to run the federal government"[391] and that Faubus was an "uneducated plow boy."[392]

As far as serving as a goodwill ambassador to Russia, Satchmo retorted, "People over there are going to ask me what's wrong with my country. What am I supposed to say?"[393] Lubenow gave Armstrong a chance to tone it down, but Pops was mad. "Don't take nothing out of that story. That's just what I said, and still say."[394] To emphasize, Louis Armstrong signed his name and wrote "solid" at the bottom of the story.[395]

He continued to stand by his comments despite what his backpedaling road manager, Pierre "Frenchie" Tallerie, indicated to the media. Tallerie said Pops was "sorry he spouted off."[396] Armstrong wouldn't have it.

"As much as I'm trying to do for my people, this road man, Tallerie… has proved that he hates Negroes. I don't see why [my manager] doesn't remove him from this band," Armstrong said. "He has done more harm than good."[397]

Pretty strong words for a performer who had reached the top of his profession and had everything to lose. Pops's activist stature has only improved over time. Trumpeter Nicholas Payton of New Orleans summed it up perfectly in 2011 when he said, "Louis bowed and scraped so Miles [Davis] could turn his back."[398]

In 1875, the Fourth of July was a Black holiday. By 1901, white people felt it was safe to celebrate Independence Day again. Reconstruction? Forgotten. Jim Crow was cranking up. World War II, the civil rights struggle, Vietnam, the Cold War, Reaganism, Clinton, 9/11, Obama, Black Lives Matter and Trump are a long way from the Emancipation Proclamation. By the time of Louis Armstrong's 100th birthday, little emotional knowledge remains of what Independence Day meant to a freedman.

But small things lingered. New Orleanians instinctively kept the meaning of Armstrong's Independence Day fire burning even if they never gave a thought to what the day meant to Satchmo. Concerts in New Orleans's Jackson Square honoring Armstrong's Fourth of July birthday began after his death in 1975 until 1986, when the New Orleans Recreation Department ran out of event money.[399]

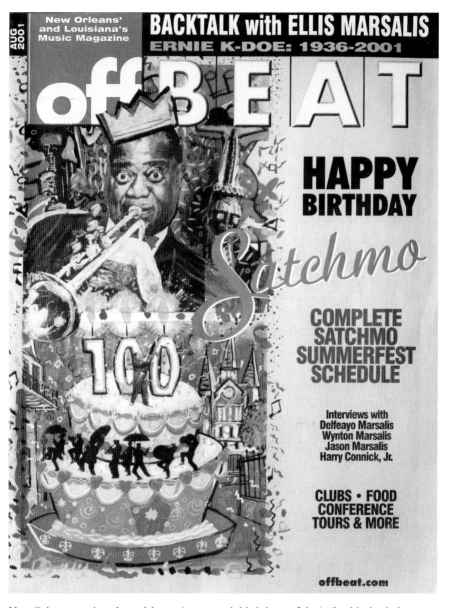

New Orleans continued to celebrate Armstrong's birthday on July 4 after his death, but when the Louisiana Department of Culture, Recreation and Tourism sponsored the first Satchmo SummerFest in August 2001, it seemed the state attached official status to the August 4 birthday. *From* Offbeat *magazine, used with permission; illustration by Richard Thomas. Image provided courtesy of the Louis Armstrong House Museum.*

Even though Tad Jones announced his bombshell birthday discovery in 1988, public recognition of Armstrong continued to focus on July 4. Birthday concerts resumed in Armstrong Park in 1987[400] and 1988.[401] In 2000, Wynton Marsalis and Leroy Jones "raised their horns in tribute to Satchmo's purported birthday."[402] There were no large public celebrations until the city honored Satchmo by renaming the airport Louis Armstrong New Orleans International Airport in 2001.[403] Then the State of Louisiana's Department of Culture, Recreation and Tourism decisively recognized the August 4 birthdate when it created the Satchmo SummerFest at the Old U.S. Mint in the French Quarter. *Picayune* writer Bruce Eggler suggested the state got behind the festival because it had "come under fire…for doing too little to celebrate the 100th anniversary of the day Louis Armstrong claimed as his birth date."[404]

The state had been interested in promoting late summer tourism in New Orleans for some time. The Louisiana Department of Culture, Recreation and Tourism had assisted Ken Burns with his *Jazz* documentary, and a fresh television audience got a glimpse of how "Armstrong changed American music forever."[405] Coincidentally, the August 4, 2001 date meshed with a previously planned University of New Orleans fundraiser concert featuring Ellis, Branford, Wynton, Delfeayo and Jason Marsalis and Harry Connick Jr. A symposium on Armstrong and jazz was also being planned by Dr. Connie Atkinson of the Midlo Center at UNO at the same time. It was easy to piggyback the three events, and the Satchmo SummerFest was born.[406]

It was now official—with state recognition, Louis Armstrong was born on August 4, 2001.

The news of the birthday shift did not sit well with trumpeter Greg Stafford, who has been performing traditional jazz for more than forty years. Stafford seemed to intrinsically understand the importance of Independence Day to Black people.

"My feeling is that people tend to dwell into the social lives of Black people and sometimes don't understand the way Black people live," Stafford said in *Offbeat* magazine.[407] He organized a second line with the Black Men of Labor Social Aid and Pleasure Club to protest.

Trumpeter Kermit Ruffins took a diplomatic and humorous approach. "I think [Armstrong] has always been one of the most blessed men in the world so maybe he should have two birthdays," he said.[408]

For years, Wynton Marsalis underappreciated Armstrong but eventually understood Pops personified "the sound of America and the freedom that it is supposed to represent."[409]

More than one hundred years after the birth of Mayann's gifted son, can twenty-first-century Americans fully understand what Independence Day meant to her generation? What did the Declaration of Independence mean to an American Revolutionary in 1776, the freedmen of 1876 and a Black musical genius born in 1901?

Did Mayann, born in 1886, ten years after Reconstruction, comprehend the injustice of her parents' slavery? Did her talented son? Were they protesting the social order by insisting fully his birthday was on the Fourth of July or simply appreciating the preciousness of their American citizenship?

Stafford, a keeper of Satchmo's flame, demurred if Louis was making a political statement.

"That's the mystery we'll never know," he said.[410]

Chapter 4

LOUIS ARMSTRONG
IN BATON ROUGE

L ouis Armstrong was a gifted trumpet player, but even the naturally talented need guides to point them in the right direction.

Some of his helpers didn't know the kid had talent; they were just doing their jobs. One was the policeman who arrested young Louis after he illegally discharged a pistol on New Year's Eve in 1912 and sent him to the Colored Waif's Home reform school. Captain Joseph Jones ran the Waif's Home with strict discipline and corporal punishment and made sure Louis followed the rules of the house. Louis's first music teacher, Peter Davis, wisely chose young Louis to be the school's brass band leader. When Kid Ory heard Louis play at just thirteen, he mentored him.

In 1922, bandleader Joe "King" Oliver, already established musically in Chicago, sent a telegram to Louis offering him a job in his band. That famous telegram got the young Satchmo to leave New Orleans for good, but perhaps the most important influencer in the talented trumpet player's life was Fate Marable. Pianist Marable was the best orchestra leader on the Streckfus Line of entertainment steamboats that plied the Mississippi River. He had been watching Louis for some time and asked the young trumpet player to join the Jazz Maniacs on the *Daisy Belle* steamboat in the spring of 1919. "We [the excursion boats] were going in and out of New Orleans all the time," Marable said. "I began to notice the type of music they were playing there. It just got under my skin."[411]

By 1919, Marable riverboat bands were composed entirely of Black musicians from New Orleans, Louis Armstrong included.

Though musically self-taught, Marable, who was of mixed race, had an impeccable reputation as a musician, especially in the Crescent City. Hired by Captain Joe Streckfus when he was just seventeen, Marable was the man on the top deck who played the steamboat's waterproof calliope keyboards to attract paying customers to the riverboat. It was a steamy, wet and loud job. The keyboard was hot to touch, so he wore gloves and a heavy oilskin raincoat and stuffed cotton in his ears. After that strenuous and wet workout, he donned a tuxedo to lead the Black musicians in the ballroom, performing six days a week for white audiences and one day for a Black audience. His musicianship qualified him to lead the Streckfus Line orchestra, but he had honed his jazz performance skills during the heyday of New Orleans's Storyville red-light district and played jam sessions with the bordello piano players Jelly Roll Morton, Tony Jackson, Calvin Jackson, Udell Wilson, Wilhelmina Bart Wynn and Edna Francis, among others.[412]

Marable taught Louis to read music, a skill that obviously played a big role in his long career. Zutty Singleton, Louis's New Orleans pal and the best early jazz drummer, said, "There was a saying in New Orleans. When some musician would get a job on the riverboats with Fate Marable, they'd say, 'Well, you're going to the conservatory.' That's because Fate was such a fine musician and the men who worked with him had to be really good."[413]

The Streckfus Steamboat Line's *Capitol* was the boat that brought Louis Armstrong to his first documented appearance in Baton Rouge on October 5, 1920, with Fate Marable's Palmetto Jazzerites. *Murphy Library Special Collections/ARC, University of Wisconsin–LaCrosse.*

Marable rehearsed the orchestra daily and taught Louis the fine art of reading music and ensemble playing during the intermissions. He also taught Louis professionalism, and the riverboat experience showed the kid how to dress and act in the larger world beyond New Orleans. Louis played excursion trips in New Orleans on the *Dixie Belle* (a swank gig), but in the spring of 1920, Marable offered Louis a chance to play the summer season. That meant the cornetist would have to leave the comfort zone of his beloved red-beans-and-rice-on-Monday New Orleans for months. Pops took the job and traveled by train to St. Louis, where he boarded the *Capitol*.

The *Capitol* made its way down the Mississippi to Baton Rouge on October 5, and Armstrong, an unknown talent, performed his first documented professional appearance in the Louisiana state capital with Marable's Palmetto Jazzerites. The boat docked at the Florida Street wharf, two blocks away from the castle-like "old" State Capitol.

Baton Rouge folks were excited to visit the boat, as the Palmetto Jazzerites had been touted as the "best bunch of syncopators in the business" by Baton Rouge's *State Times*:

> *Dance fans of this community will be given a real treat Tuesday October 5. For rhythm and melody the Palmetto Jazzerites are beyond compare for they are in a class by themselves and everybody that hears them play is loud in acclaiming it the best bunch of syncopators in the business. Real jazz originated in the southland with the strumming of the banjos on the plantation and it is a peculiar sort of melody that is very pleasing when properly played by real artists. It is next to impossible to keep your feet quiet when you hear the Palmetto Jazzerites play the popular dance numbers.*[414]

In addition to the nineteen-year-old Louis Armstrong, the Palmetto Jazzerites also included Boyd Adkins (clarinet, saxophone and violin), Norman Brashear (trombone), "Baby" Dodds (drums), David Jones (saxophone), Henry Kimball (string bass) and Johnny St. Cyr (banjo).[415]

Fate Marable and the experience he provided prepared Louis Armstrong for a long professional career. Marable had an eye and ear for talent, as evidenced by the "graduates" of his "conservatory," many of whom went on to play with notable bandleaders like Cab Calloway, Count Basie, Duke Ellington, Fats Waller, Chick Webb and Clark Terry.[416]

The 1920 *Capitol* show was the first documented Baton Rouge appearance of Louis Armstrong, but Joe Darensbourg, born in 1906, said he first saw Louis play in the Firemen's Parade as early as circa 1918 on North Boulevard.

The Baton Rouge Pelican Hook and Ladder Company No. 1 with their decorated ladder wagon at a firemen's parade. Baton Rouge did not have much of a Mardi Gras parade tradition, but clarinetist Joe Darensbourg said Papa Celestin's Tuxedo Band often traveled to perform in the city's firemen's parades and funerals. Darensbourg said he recognized Louis Armstrong's parade playing as early as 1918. *LSU Libraries, Special Collections.*

The Darensbourg home on North Boulevard was on the parade route. "Every parade that passed in Baton Rouge, passed in front of my house," Darensbourg said. "The shoe shop was in the front, and we lived in the house in the back. I'm standing along the curb with a lot of kids, watching this music go by, with the different little floats."[417]

As the parade rolled nearer to the Darensbourg shoe shop, Darensbourg began to identify the musicians he knew, but he didn't know Louis. He quickly became acquainted with his sound. "We heard this trumpet, this cornet," Joe said. "When I heard that thing, you couldn't believe it. Nobody asked, 'Where's Louis?' in Baton Rouge. I think that was the first time he had come to Baton Rouge."[418]

The crowd was fascinated with the sounds the kid in the red hat was making. Darensbourg recalled the group conversation:

> *Who is playing that cornet? What is that instrument? A guy said, "It sounds like a cornet. But nobody can play like that." So finally, as they're*

marching, Louis had that horn up there with that little old red hat on, just blowing up a breeze. He's got his little head up there, overpowering everybody. When they got by, we were going to light out. But before, some guy in the back of me, he's a railroad porter on a train, he says, "I know what that is. They call him Dipper. His name is Louis Armstrong. I know who he is," the guy kept saying. "I know him!" In the meantime, we're gone, making that second line right behind him.[419]

The young Darensbourg said that hearing Louis in that North Boulevard parade was "one [of] the thrills" of his life.[420] "This was the first time I seen Louis; this was before I ever knew who he was. You could hear that damn cornet two blocks away—I never heard a cornet like it. I'll never forget it. That's one of the things that really made me want to be a musician, hearing a sound like that. What a man!" Darensbourg said.[421]

Darensbourg was probably twelve years old when he first heard Louis Armstrong on North Boulevard in front of his family's shoe shop. He made a promise to himself that he would one day play with Louis Armstrong, and he did.

And what a gig it was. He played clarinet on "Hello, Dolly," Armstrong's number-one hit. While touring with Louis from 1961 to 1963, they played nearly every country in the world except the Soviet Union.

Chapter 5

WE'RE GOING TO GIVE BASIN STREET
BACK ITS NAME!

For jazz lovers, Basin Street, New Orleans, is one of the most famous streets in the world. It was the inspiration for "Basin Street Blues," a jazz tune written by composer Spencer Williams in 1926. The song is one of the anthems of New Orleans and considered a jazz standard.[422] It was the seventy-ninth most recorded tune in the first half of the twentieth century[423] and is one of the most recognizable and recorded songs ever.[424] Every jazz band and every great singer of that era and beyond have performed and recorded it. It's in the repertoire of every traditional jazz band throughout the world.

The song made New Orleans famous, so why did the city fathers of the Crescent City rename it North Saratoga Street in 1921?[425]

When Louis Armstrong was born in 1901, Basin Street was the back o' town boundary. Back o' town was not a nice neighborhood. It was where poor Black people lived. They were unsophisticated and labeled as "ratty" people. Basin Street parallels Rampart Street and runs five blocks from Canal Street down past St. Louis Cemetery. Today, it turns toward Lake Pontchartrain and merges into Orleans Avenue.

New Orleans, known for its *bon vivant* atmosphere, was long occupied by federal troops during and after the Civil War. Those bivouacked soldiers went home and spread the gospel of the Mississippi River town. Historian Joe Gray Taylor cited a North Carolinian's letter to a friend extolling New Orleans:

I felicitate you on your pleasant trip to New Orleans….But I was surprised to hear of such abounding good cheer. I had figured to myself N.O. as a perfect pandemonium, at least to good old Confederates—and that one of their torments would be to see all the good things you speak of in the clutches of the carpetbaggers—while they would have to content themselves with the smell of the cooking and aroma of the wines. I am glad to know there is one place at least where a Confederate gentleman can live as he desires to do.[426]

Presumably, Union soldiers wrote to their comrades about New Orleans as well.

Like every large city, New Orleans had problems with prostitution, and the mansions of Basin Street had become the busiest whorehouse district in the world outside of Paris by 1870. Two years before the turn of the twentieth century, Alderman Sidney Story successfully pushed for a district that would contain the brothels in a sixteen-block area. The media, always eager to call out politicians, quickly dubbed the prostitution district "Storyville." (Jazz chronicler Danny Barker said residents always referred to Storyville as the "district.")[427] From 1898 through 1917, Basin Street was the lakeside boundary of the prostitution district.[428] The street, lined with high-end saloons, cabarets, gambling dens and opulent mansions that housed dozens of prostitutes, was the entrance to a semi-official demimonde.

As the United States entered World War I, the War Department increased its funding to its Algiers-based navy yard, an important economic driver for the city. Congress also passed a new war effort law creating buffer zones banning houses of prostitution around military bases to protect soldiers from venereal disease. As Storyville had justifiably earned a national reputation as one of the "worst vice districts in the United States,"[429] it quickly came under attack by the law's policing Commission on Training Camp Activities. The CTCA labeled Storyville "a veritable Mecca of whores."[430] Though the city temporarily exploited a congressional oversight (a failure to include sailors in the legislation), the navy threatened to close the base. On November 12, 1917, at midnight, Storyville was shut down.

Gone, but not forgotten, past Storyville customers were nostalgically reminded of their visits to the infamous district after Basin Street became famous in song seven years later when composer Spencer Williams published a simple twelve-bar chorus and called it "Basin Street Blues."[431]

It is believed that Williams, an Alabama native, spent time in New Orleans as a teenager at his aunt Lulu White's brothel, the famous/infamous Mahogany Hall, and had fond remembrances of Basin Street and Storyville.

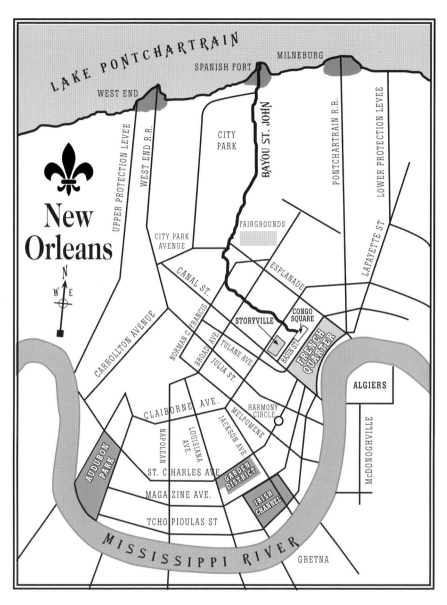

Basin Street in New Orleans is one of the most famous streets in the world, especially to jazz lovers. City fathers, however, were embarrassed by the lewdness the street represented as the gateway to Storyville, the city's legal red-light district from 1898 to 1917. The city, eager to erase the memory of Storyville, changed the name of Basin Street to the unglamorous North Saratoga Street in 1921. *Map by Gene Hansen.*

Williams had already traveled through the Deep South, Chicago, New York and Paris, where he was friend to Josephine Baker, an American-born French singer, actress and dancer with the *Folies Bergère*. He had hits with "Tishomingo Blues," "I Ain't Gonna Give Nobody None of This Jelly Roll," "Royal Garden Blues" and "Arkansas Blues." He was one of the earliest Black members of the American Society of Composers and Performers (ASCAP).[432] Jazz historian Gary Giddins called Williams the "Bard of Basin Street."[433]

New Orleans native Louis Armstrong, who had firmly established himself as an American musical star at age twenty-six, recorded the song two years later, and the tune peaked on the record charts at number twenty.[434] The intro to Pops's version sounded like a fairy tale. To get the soft, ethereal mix, Earl Hines played a celesta and Louis followed with a trumpet solo and scat singing. Bandmates Fred Robinson and Jimmy Strong backed him up with choir-like humming.

With the trendsetting Pops covering the tune, "Basin Street Blues" was well on its way to becoming a jazz standard. For nearly one hundred years, performers like Willie Nelson, Wynton Marsalis, Ray Charles, Miles Davis, Dr. Michael White, Ella Fitzgerald, Harry Connick Jr., Sam Cooke, Benny Goodman, Bing Crosby and Connie Boswell, Dr. John, Louis Prima, Pete Fountain, Fats Waller, Big Bad Voodoo Daddy, David Sanborn, Preservation Hall Jazz Band, Dave Brubeck, Dean Martin, Asleep at the Wheel and Kid Koala have covered the song.

Cab Calloway's twelve-bar version, recorded on July 9, 1931, featured his famous scatting and Reuben Reeves's trumpet solo played in the "Armstrong manner."[435] In February 1931, the song got a major workover by trombonist Jack Teagarden and arranger Glenn Miller. They were part of Columbia Records' Charleston Chasers, the label's jazz group. Teagarden and Miller (also a trombonist) wrote an introductory verse with the famous line, "Won't you come along with me down the Mississippi?" that set the tune in stone.

The Chasers were a studio-only ensemble from 1925 to 1931 that featured various jazzmen, including Red Nichols (trumpet), Jimmy Dorsey (clarinet), Tommy Dorsey (trombone), Benny Goodman (clarinet) and Gene Krupa (drums).[436] The Miller/Teagarden group was the last to record under the Charleston Chasers name, and their session featuring Teagarden's vocals made an indelible stamp on the history of "Basin Street Blues" and "guaranteed the band's immortality" with jazz lovers.[437]

Arranger Miller, nervous about the recording session, called Teagarden the night before the group was due in the studio. "Jack, I think we could do a better job if we could put together some lyrics and you could sing it. Want to come over and see what we can do?" Teagarden said. "We finally finished the job sometime early in the morning. Next day, we cut the record. It's been the most popular I've ever done! The lyrics were later included with the sheet music, but it never carried our names."[438]

In 1943, when Teagarden's big band was playing the St. Charles Theater in New Orleans, he told the *Times-Picayune* that "Basin Street Blues" was his most requested song by the "army and navy boys in the service camps,"[439] but the origin of the song remained a mystery to him.

"We were never able to discover the real origin of the song but since we put our version on paper, copies and recording of the number have sold in the millions. Boys in the service camps and posts ask us for 'Basin' more than for any other number."[440]

The white Teagarden, born in northeast Texas, where his mother was a ragtime pianist, was well versed in the Black influence on church music, blues and jazz. He may have well thought "Basin Street Blues" was out there so long it was traditional. In 1931, it appears the song was part of the standard repertoire and recorded many times and heard thousands of times on the radio. A young Judy Garland loved the song.

Before *The Wizard of Oz* became a hit movie, in 1938, twelve-year-old Judy Garland was a blossoming singer/actor promoting her new movie *Everybody Sing* and making a whirlwind "tween-trains" stop in New Orleans while en route to Miami. *Times-Picayune* writer Cleveland Sessums interviewed the young actor in a police-escorted car ride on her way to the Louisville and Nashville depot.

"[New Orleans] reminds me of San Francisco," Garland said as she viewed the city from her window. "I want to see Canal Street and where is Basin Street? The 'Basin Street Blues' is a swell song."[441]

No doubt Judy had heard "Basin Street Blues" many times.

Since her car was being driven on Canal Street, Judy got her first wish. Arriving at the L&N station, she was greeted by E.A. Farley of the New Orleans Florists' Association, who presented her with a bouquet of Philippine orchids. The local movie theater managers and autograph seekers were also at the station. On the train, Garland and her mother were served champagne and a Creole breakfast from Chef Roy Alciatore of Antoine's. The "eager and interested youngster with an unusual ability" declined the alcohol.[442]

And what of her desire to see the "swell" Basin Street? Sessums wrote that "limited time prevented anything but a musical exploration of Basin Street."[443]

In 1938, Judy Garland wasn't even a teenager. She knew she wasn't allowed to sip champagne even if it was being served to her by a renowned New Orleans chef. The young star was "eager," said "thank you" and promoted the studio like a pro. Despite all the acclaim, according to Sessums, "she [was] still herself."[444]

So why were the Crescent City adults who met young Judy at the train station reluctant to show her Basin Street?

Because that's where the whorehouses were. Or, more accurately, had been. And the street was gone.

In 1938, Basin Street no longer existed on New Orleans city maps. Despite the famous song, New Orleans had not had a Basin Street for seventeen years.

The street name was abolished on May 4, 1921, by City Commissioner of Public Property Wilbert Black because the name was "linked closely with the old 'red light' district's history and is a reminder of 'the old days.'"[445] The "old days" referred to the period from 1898 to 1917 when more than two thousand prostitutes sold their sexual services in Storyville. Mayor Andrew McShane, elected in 1920, was a reform candidate and a "life-long enemy of the New Orleans ring,"[446] the organization that tolerated the district in the young twentieth century.

In reality, the Basin Street in Judy Garland's mind, where white and Black people freely mingled, never existed in Jim Crow New Orleans.[447] Basin Street was the boundary of the district created by the city council on January 1, 1898, to contain and limit prostitution.

Why was this necessary? By the 1850s, prostitution was a big problem in the Crescent City. New Orleans had been made wealthy by the slave-born agrarian economy of sugar cane, and the municipal government began taking steps to curtail the less desirable activity that came with that wealth.

At the founding of the colony, King Louis XIV and Louis XV of France allowed the transport of "many dozens of, and indeed hundreds, of prostitutes and other disreputable women" to Louisiana as early as 1715. From 1718 to 1720, colonial entrepreneur John Law's Mississippi Company was known to have allowed the kidnapping of innumerable "gypsies" and "women of bad repute" to ship off to the New World as "colonists." There were respectable people among them, but there were also "prostitutes, thieves, vagabonds, and every other kind of wretch." Bienville, the founder of the city, understated when he said many of the women, who had been taken from "a house of corruption" in Paris, "had not been well selected."[448]

For more than one hundred years, the people who built the French Quarter had been excavating dirt from the back o' town to aid in building their homes, businesses and streets.[449] A large pond was eventually created. Governor Francisco Luis Hector de Carondelet, realizing that urban drainage was a serious issue (what a surprise!) in New Orleans, built the Canal Carondelet to improve drainage and connect to Lake Pontchartrain. The canal went into service in 1796.[450]

In ensuing years, as Spanish Louisiana was horse traded to France and then to the United States, Mayor James Pitot improved the canal by building towpaths on either side of the canal guide levees so mules could pull barges. Docks were built around the inland-turning basin, and Basin Street was born. The harlots built shacks near the basin and along the canal, hung out red lanterns and, *voila*, Basin Street, as a center for prostitution, was created.[451]

Andrew Jackson successfully defended the city against British invasion in 1814, and the town, now safely American and part of the United States, saw an increase in river traffic, which brought "riotous crews of rough and rowdy rivermen fresh off the boats, eager for whiskey and women, and with money in their pockets."[452]

Eventually, railroads were built paralleling the canal. The Southern Railroad, built in 1908, turned on to Basin Street, running up the "neutral ground" (as street medians are called locally) to one of the city's main railroad depots on Canal Street.

But prostitution was not content to stay in the basin. As New Orleans expanded, so did the brothels, dance halls, cockfighting pits, saloons and rooming houses. The trouble folks get into when they whore, drink and gamble followed on the heels of vice. A six-block "Swamp" (present-day O'Keefe and down Girod Street to the Warehouse and Lower Garden District)[453] became notorious. A customer could visit the Swamp and purchase a woman, bed and whiskey for a picayune (a six-cent coin). If a customer didn't have more money with him than he was willing to part with, he often made it out of the Swamp alive. There were eight hundred known murders in the Swamp between 1820 and 1850.[454] The policing authorities didn't do much patrolling there.

And it got worse. Prostitution expanded across the city thanks to the gold rush. The steady stream of customers dwindled to a trickle after gold was discovered in California in 1849. Hookers packed up and went west, but the remaining whores, starved for customers, infiltrated the "American Quarter" (the Garden District and Irish Channel),[455] the two blocks of Gallatin Street ("that quiet, respectable thoroughfare")[456] and "Sanctity Row," located around the intersection of present-day Elysian Fields Avenue and North St. Peters Street.

Incidents of depravity and violence were not anecdotal during the 1850s on Gallatin Street. "The frail daughters of Gallatin" and the "good and true [men] of Gallatin Street" proved time and time again that there was "no redeeming feature to this street of streets."[457]

"City Intelligence," the Times-Picayune's police blotter column, reported that Bill Clark "assaulted Marie Gervais, in Gallatin street, and seized her violently by the neck, without any just cause or provocation."[458] "Thomas Burns, alias Bonniard, a resident of Gallatin street…stabbed Wm. Mason in the neck…without cause or provocation. He is well known to the police of the Second District."[459] "Mary Ann Kelly was arrested at the request of Wm. Finley…in Gallatin street, charged with robbing him of $50."[460] "Two men…Leandro Silvan and Narciso Ponche were arrested…charged with attempting to assassinate Peter Johnson in his own house, No. 11 Gallatin street. Silvan had a bowie knife concealed on his person at the time of his arrest."[461] America Williams, "the world's strongest whore,"[462] was charged with "hammering" another woman.[463]

By 1865, the Picayune seemed tired of reporting Gallatin mayhem and was reduced to making up new words to describe killing: "Alas, that our pen should be called on to mention so many murders. But murder is the most ancient of crimes, and then it appeared in the form of fratricide. We have now a case of gunicide, if we can be allowed to coin a word."[464]

Tulane University geographer Richard Campanella posited the reason Gallatin Street "formed the highest concentration of illegal sex, drinking, violence, robberies, pickpockets and scams in antebellum New Orleans" was because it was at the periphery of the busy open-air French Market, populated with "stalls, conveyances, errand-runners, day-hires, cheap food, running water, amusements, customers round-the-clock, and cash in every pocket" that attracted "loiter[er]s, transients, curiosity-seekers and adventurers," obviously the patrons that bars, brothels and gambling houses sought.[465] It was also near the U.S. Mint, a factory with environmental hazards, the international shipping wharfs at the foot of Esplanade and the Pontchartrain Railroad station on Elysian Fields. Campanella noted the area "had all the right ingredients for a vice district: access, anonymity, low rents, cheap eats, a quick buck and strangers coming and going at all hours."[466]

City hall could not prevent homicide, but maybe it could prevent the world's oldest profession from being New Orleans's largest. Previous laws—

like the 1817 ordinance calling for a twenty-five-dollar fine or thirty days imprisonment for women "notoriously abandoned to lewdness" and the 1837 measure allowing any three respectable citizens to sign a petition and empowering the mayor to evict whores—were not enforced because they were unenforceable. But the 1857 "Ordinance Concerning Lewd and Abandoned Women," dubbed the "Lorette Law" after the French slang for "whores," had a chance.

The Lorette Law regulated sex work by taxing prostitutes $100 and brothel keepers $250. It applied only to certain municipal geographic areas and provided that the sex workers could not occupy any one-story building or the lower floor of any structure. They could not "stand upon the sidewalk… or at the alley way, door or gate…nor sit upon the steps [with] an indecent posture [nor] stroll about the streets of the city indecently attired." White and "free colored" prostitutes could not occupy the same house, and public women were banned from soliciting customers in cabarets or coffeehouses. It was a novel idea: license the prostitutes and make the profession taxable in a limited area.[467]

Gallatin Street's "numerous and chaste nymphs of that poetic region"[468] weren't going to have it. They brought their case all the way to the Louisiana Supreme Court, which ruled in their favor in 1859. Hundreds of whores celebrated in a vulgar public manner by parading via carriage up and down Canal Street, through the French Quarter, "gesturing obscenely, displaying themselves, insulting shocked housewives, and otherwise calling attention to the triumph of the sin industry."[469]

City fathers passed eight new versions of the Lorette Law over the next forty years, and all were struck down, but there was a loophole. The Lorette Law never included the lake side of Basin Street in the Canal-Toulouse and Customhouse-Franklin Streets. The ladies of back o' town were able to practice their trade relatively unscathed by authorities while other locations were subject to police interference. Hence, the foundation for Storyville was built.[470]

Despite the Lorette Law, the dubious constitutionality of restrictions did little to control vice in the Crescent City, and ostentatious tales of madams and their lovers only enhanced New Orleans's reputation as a sin city and the location of political hanky-panky.

State Senator James D. Beares, the lover of Hattie Hamilton who helped her build the "most magnificent of the *maison d'amours*"[471] at 21 South Basin Street, was so corrupt that the first question anyone asked when doing business with the state was, "Where does Beares come in?"[472]

An undercover reporter, "a certain one of the silent shadows," was once escorted by an unidentified "Captain" down Gallatin Street and later to the Twenty-One, Hattie's house of sin. The reporter described the house as one of "noble proportions, of a dark red hue, and whose aristocratic tint doubtless served as a fitting prelude to the architectural glories within."[473]

Impressed, the informant, eloquently tongue in cheek, noted:

> *This place looks too magnificent to be precisely a private residence. Or if it is one, it is such as a grateful nation ought to give to her ablest son, to her bravest General, her most virtuous statesman or best reporter. Is it possible that a distinguished General or banker resides here?*
>
> *No (the Captain replied), They only come as visitors.*[474]

Hamilton's well-connected state senator directed wealthy clients to the Twenty-One, and she was able to charge fifty dollars for trysts at the house.[475] Her downfall and ultimate bankruptcy began when she was suspected of killing Beares in 1870.

The *Picayune* reported:

> *He was shot on Friday night, accidentally it is alleged, while capping a pistol. There are, of course, widely various impressions concerning the manner in which the fatal shot was fired. He had been living for some time with Hattie Hamilton, a woman formerly the proprietress of a disreputable house on Basin street. She even passed as his wife and was held out to the community in which they immediately resided as such. It is said they had been quarreling the evening preceding the occurrence, and one or two shots were fired, but by whom it was impossible to ascertain, inasmuch as the woman and Senator Beares were alone in the room, as they were at the time of the fatal shooting. It was several minutes before the servants were aware of the occurrence.*[476]

Murder, stabbings, suicide attempts and shootings were regular occurrences on Gallatin Street, Smoky Row and Basin Street, but Kate Townsend's 1883 murder at the hands of her Creole fancy man, Troisville Sykes, became the "most widely publicized sex murder in New Orleans history."[477]

Townsend's name was no stranger to the newspaper. Bits of salacious information about her dotted the city's media throughout the 1860s and '70s. Dealing with threats at 40 Basin Street, her Maison Dorée, was a way of life for the rich New Orleans madam. Over the course of twenty years, she managed to accumulate an estate of more than $90,000 ($3 million in 2022 dollars). A man threatening her life was nothing new. She had one Edward Murphy arrested in 1869 for "disturbing the peace and threatening to take her life."

But on the night of November 3, 1883, "a most shocking and horrible tragedy startled that portion of the city on Basin street occupied by members of the demimonde. Kate Townsend, who reigned queen of the frail sisterhood for many years, and who was probably known in every quarter of the land, was killed—murdered by [Troisville] Sykes."[478]

It was a lovers' quarrel, Sykes said, as he declared self-defense. Charged with murder, he was acquitted and subsequently claimed Townsend's estate based on a will he produced. Ultimately, he won the court case but walked away with only thirty dollars.[479]

Whorehouses had been a fact of life in New Orleans since colonial times, but because of its Mississippi River trade route, the city grew rapidly and became wealthy. In 1840, it was the third-largest city in the country and one of the richest.[480] Wealth brought respectability. Since prostitution was tolerated anywhere in New Orleans on the second floors and above, a rising middle-class property owner (or wealthy banker) was afraid a madam would set up shop next door.

"These women, with few exceptions, made little or no effort to conduct their affairs discreetly or to exhibit a decent respect for the sensibilities of their respectable neighbors," wrote Al Rose in his *Storyville, New Orleans: Being an Authentic, Illustrated Account of the Notorious Red-Light District*. "They seemed to take a certain pleasure in flaunting their viciousness."[481]

A new muckraking weekly, the *Mascot*, began to publish sordid tales of how vice affected property value. The decent citizens also learned that the city was full of unregulated "labor agencies" that sold virgins for up to $800. The *Mascot* even threatened to reveal the names of men who participated in the "Ball of the Two Well Known Gentlemen," a Mardi Gras for "pimps, procurers, prostitutes, petty politicians and police."[482]

The city's elite clamored for a solution. The Townsend-Sykes case reinforced the weariness with the city's prostitution, crime rates, various epidemics and distinct racial climate. The intentional focus of media on the negative aspects of New Orleans life created a negative view of the city centered on immorality and exasperated by sensational crimes like Townsend's murder.[483]

Reformers like alderman Sidney Story believed prostitution could and should be regulated. Other reformers believed that America's "republican

The *Mascot* scandal sheet focused a lot of attention on the social issues of nineteenth-century New Orleans, including sex trafficking. Despite the racially stereotyped caricatures of Black people, this 1890 cover may have been the first to illustrate a jazz band. Some refined folks did not like jazz and blamed it for "the heart attack of an elderly classical cornetist, an unfavorable trade balance between the United States and Hungary, the waning quality of Italian tenors, the frightening of bears in Siberia and the decline of modern civilization." *City Archives and Special Collections, New Orleans Public Library.*

institutions and economic opportunity"[484] would cause the oldest profession to wither away. But the prevailing attitude of the time was that "sexual intercourse was vital to men's mental and physical health."[485] To keep that need in check, Alderman Story and a prominent New Orleans attorney named Thomas McCaleb Hyman researched whorehouses in Europe and wrote up an ordinance noting:

> *It shall be unlawful for any public prostitute or woman notoriously abandoned to lewdness to occupy, inhabit, live or sleep in any house, room or closet situated without the following limits: South side of Customhouse street from Basin to Robertson street, east side of Robertson street from Customhouse to Saint Louis street, from Robertson to Basin street.*[486]

The measure passed on January 29, 1897.[487]

Prior to the creation of the district, it was feared a whorehouse could set up shop in any respectable neighborhood. The district eliminated that fear, so everyone was happy. Well, two property owners were not happy: George L'Hote and the Church Extension Society. L'Hote owned a home a half block from the district. The church society represented the Black congregation of the Methodist Episcopal Church on Bienville Street. They rightly fought the constitutional legality of the district all the way up to the United States Supreme Court. The same court that gave us the *Plessy v. Ferguson* "separate but legal" doctrine ruled against L'Hote and the Black Methodist Episcopalians.[488]

Another group that was dissatisfied with the creation of Storyville were the prostitutes who had established houses in other parts of New Orleans. They either had to move their operations to the district or face prosecution. Some shut down altogether and moved out of the city. But many moved back after they learned of the advantages of practicing their trade in a protected district.

Author Al Rose interviewed one such whore who had moved to Galveston to work but returned to New Orleans three months after the district was created:

> *I thought the District was gonna be like a big house of correction, where the "peelers" would be like stir guard—you know—you'd be all the time under their thumb—who wants that? So, I got out to Galveston where the cops lay off, but the tricks is cheap—sailors and roustabouts. Anyhow, I begin to hear how great it is for workin' girls, and so I come back and rented a crib*

on Conti Street for three dollars a day. I started off charging a buck and I remember the first week I took in over a hundred dollars—which was the most I ever made in my life up to that time.[489]

The newspapers quickly dubbed the red-light district "Storyville," which reportedly upset Alderman Story. Banjoist Danny Barker, born in 1909, said the residents and service people always referred to the area as "the district,"[490] but the newspapers never passed up a chance to call it Storyville. If there was a fire in the district, it was headlined, "Storyville Blaze."[491] If it was a matter of policing, a headline might read, "Storyville Injunction Makes Law Officers Hesitate."[492] A man who was just "taking in the sights"[493] of the district but was waylaid and robbed produced a "Saw Storyville" report.[494] At some point, Sidney Story must have regretted the law of unintentional consequences.

Even in his lifetime, New Orleans native Al Rose (1916–1993) ruminated that "Storyville remains enshrined in myth, romance and nostalgia" in his 1974 book, *Storyville, New Orleans*.[495]

The area that had been Storyville was off-limits to me as a child, but I did catch occasional glimpses of its surviving structures. I suppose I was eight or nine years of age before I understood what prostitution was and, with my strict Roman Catholic education, I was sure it was something very nasty. Nevertheless, I couldn't fail to notice that many of the adults around me seemed to recall Storyville, "the District," with a certain nostalgia. It became for me a legend of mystery and better times.[496]

But for the two thousand prostitutes working[497] in the district, it was anything but enigmatic. For the sex workers, no matter the hyperbole about the glamorous mansions on Basin Street gilded with gold, it was a matter of economics. Women, like Black people, had few educational and business opportunities, and many became whores primarily because of hunger. Other reasons could involve financial problems or lure of easy money.[498] It was rare for a woman with insatiable sexual appetites to be drawn into the profession, and those who did were generally looked down on. Madam Nell Kimball wrote in her autobiography, "I never cared much for the girl who came to work in a house because it was fun for her."[499]

The workplace could be either a high-class parlor house or "crib." The parlor houses and cribs located south of Liberty Street were white clientele only and pricier. The houses and cribs between Liberty and Villeré Streets were occupied and frequented by both races. The section between Villeré and Robertson Streets was the Black section. This section charged the lowest prices, had the roughest clientele and had numerous street walkers doing back-alley trade. The young woman from Galveston mentioned previously had over one hundred partners in a week.

Despite the Blue Books—the directories that listed each prostitute and her specialties—the opulence of the brothel mansions and the colorful names (Crying Emma, Gold Tooth Gussie, Big Butt Annie, Coke Eyed Laura, Black Sis, Buck Tooth Rena and Fast Black),[500] a life of prostitution was a miserable one. Depression and suicide were problems. Madam Nell Kimball reported, "A lot crack up and go low down blues, and some even take the deep six [suicide]. I never knew an always cheerful, golden hearted, always laughing whore. It was a life regular as sunrise: regular joy, misery, hope, lack of hope, and ideas of suicide. A shrug-off of the present, a numb idea of the future, too. We all lied to each other about the future, and to ourselves as well."[501]

Venereal disease was a fact of life, and medical care was limited. The whores themselves were the best diagnosticians of venereal disease. "Big casino" (syphilis) and "little casino" (gonorrhea) were common and deadly in an age when the "cures" were ineffective.[502]

And while the district contained the whorehouses, it didn't mean the respectable folks of New Orleans liked it. Before Storyville, Basin Street was a "high class residential street," wrote Herman H. Diers of Washington, D.C., to the editor of *Metronome* magazine. "Then [in 1908] the Southern Railway came up the center of the street, leaving just a narrow street on either side,"[503] where passengers disembarked at the Terminal Station, within feet of the brothels.

What luck. The undesirable, swampy back o' town of New Orleans's border of Basin Street where St. Louis Cemetery is located (who wants to live next door to a graveyard?) now became the "other side of the tracks."

The train tracks provided another way for the ever-resourceful harlots of Basin Street to advertise their fleshy goods. Arriving by train at the Southern Depot, from the train window, a visitor could see the mansions of Basin Street and scantily clad, even naked women, displaying their earthly delights to the men on the trains.[504] Arriving wives and mothers must have averted their eyes and those of their children to the whores' lascivious gestures. How does a society New Orleanian explain the district to genteel relatives and distinguished guests arriving by train? Must have been quite the conversation.

The business side of prostitution was devoid of glamour, however, and many customers felt like they were on a human assembly line. The prostitutes' "garishness and theatrics could not hide the base reality of their business."[505] One man about town explained, "Storyville whores, no matter how well-dressed or how gaudily expensive the whorehouse, were avaricious, greedy and uncouth."[506]

The pimps, bar owners, landlords and gamblers also contributed to the squalor of Storyville, and violence was a regular occurrence in the streets. Young Louis Armstrong witnessed a knife fight between two prostitutes named Mary Jack the Bear and Deborah who argued over their shared pimp's affection.

As soon as Deborah hit the sidewalk, Mary Jack whipped out a bylow, a big knife with a large blade. She leapt upon Deborah and started cutting up and down her face. Deborah pulled the same kind of knife and went to work on Mary Jack the Bear. The crowd was terrified and did not dare to go near them. Mary Jack the Bear died later and Deborah [survived]…but her face is marked up so badly that it looks like a scoreboard.[507]

On the positive side, Storyville did play a role in the development of jazz. The nightclubs, bars and cabarets hired musicians to attract drinkers, dancers, women, gamblers and sailors. The whorehouses also featured some top-quality pianists like Tony Jackson and Jelly Roll Morton, who played for tips.

The teenaged Morton, inexperienced in the ways of the district, was coaxed to fill in on piano in a brothel by his friends. He made twenty dollars in tips in one hour. He was reluctant to accept the money because he was "not taught that way."[508]

But Jelly Roll was a quick study:

The streets were crowded with men. Police were always in sight, never less than two together, which guaranteed the safety of all concerned. Lights of all colors were glittering and glaring. Music was pouring into the streets from every house. Women were standing in the doorways, singing or chanting some kind of blues—some very happy, some very sad, some with the desire to end it all by poison, some planning a big outing, a dance, or some other kind of enjoyment. Some were real ladies in spite of their downfall and some were habitual drunkards and some were dope fiends as follows, opium, heroin, cocaine, laudanum, morphine, etcetera. I was

"DOWN THE LINE"- Iberville, looking down Basin Street.

Tom Anderson, the unofficial mayor of Storyville, allowed prostitute Josie Arlington ("one of the most irascible bawds in the city—a considerable accomplishment, given the competition") to operate her Arlington Annex brothel above his "saloon, tourist bureau, informal city hall, and courthouse" at the corner of Basin and Iberville. City officials dealt with the district through Anderson. *New Orleans Jazz Museum.*

personally sent to Chinatown many times with a sealed note and a small amount of money and would bring back several cards of hop. There was no slipping and digging. All you had to do was walk in to be served.[509]

The list of musicians compiled by Al Rose who played in Storyville music halls and cabarets is extensive. It includes Sidney Bechet, Wellman Braud (string bass and violin), Buddy Bolden, Oscar "Papa" Celestin (trumpet), Louis Delisle "Big Eye" Nelson (trombone), brothers Johnny (clarinet) and Warren "Baby" Dodds (drums), Frankie Duson (valve trombone), George "Pops" Foster (tuba, string bass), Maurice French (trombone), Tony Jackson, Bunk Johnson, Freddie Keppard (trumpet), Jelly Roll Morton, Joe "King" Oliver, Edward "Kid" Ory, Roy Palmer (trombone), Alphonse Picou (clarinet), Armand Piron (violin), Johnny St. Cyr (banjo, guitar), Lorenzo Tio Jr. (clarinet), Louis "Papa" Tio (clarinet) and Clarence Williams (piano).

Performing in Storyville was arduous work. Many played from 8:00 p.m. to 4:00 a.m. and beyond, but the district allowed them a "relatively uncritical audience…one that permitted the musician almost unlimited freedom to experiment and to work out stylistic qualities of their own in circumstances less demanding than those experienced by performers in other milieus."[510]

Storyville also broke down the barriers between the lighter-skinned Creoles of color and their darker competitors. Jazz was first played in the open air by brass bands performing at lawn parties and the numerous New Orleans fraternal organizations' parades before the creation of Storyville, but the district attracted the best musicians, no matter if they were trained light-skinned Creoles or dark, musically illiterate Uptown Black people, because the gigs were regular.[511]

"Bolden cause all that," said fiddler Paul Dominguez. "He cause these younger Creoles, men like Bechet and Keppard, to have a different style altogether from the old heads like Tio and Perez. I don't know how they do it. But goddam, they'll do it. Can't tell you what's on the paper, but just play the hell out of it."[512]

The "old head," Louis "Papa" Tio, had never embraced the new music called jazz. After performing all over the country with the Georgia Minstrels and Excelsior Brass Band and dabbling in composing and serious performance, his tastes leaned heavily toward the European ideal. Musicians went to him for lessons. A person of color, now lumped in with the darker people of color because of the *Plessy v. Ferguson* ruling, he was descended from one of the earliest Spanish settlers of New Orleans and a French officer. His sophisticated ear was trained and knew the difference between a note in tune and a bent note. There was a cultural divide between musicians like Papa Tio and Buddy Bolden.

"Papa Tio was the old man," said cornetist Anatie "Natty" Dominique. "Well, that's a man that never liked jazz at all….He'd hear jazz and [would] run in your house, under the bed. 'Let me get under the bed! Listen to that, those fools, just messing up good music.' [If he heard jazz] anywhere in the street, he'd run in your house. He didn't like that."[513]

Buddy Bolden had already "blowed his top";[514] been committed to the mental hospital in Jackson, Louisiana; and was removed from the New Orleans music scene when Natty Dominque would have known Papa Tio, but Tio was in his prime when Bolden ascended to the trumpet throne. He knew what Bolden played. He knew it was different, and he didn't like it, but the public did. Class ranking may have also played a role in Tio's perception of Bolden.

Before the Great Migration of the 1930s, there was a migration from the cane fields to the Crescent City. Pops Foster, a non-Creole from McCall, Ascension Parish, and part of the Louisiana rural diaspora, was playing professionally just a year after Bolden "went crazy."[515] He recognized the social friction.

> *There was Uptown, Downtown and back o' town. The Downtown boys, the Creoles, thought they were better than anybody else and wouldn't hire the Uptown boys. Most of the guys who played the district were from Downtown. Some of the Downtown bands were the Imperial Band, the Superior Band, and the Olympic Band. The Uptown musicians had the biggest names, Buddy Bolden's band and Kid Ory's Band. Bolden had the biggest name around there for a long time.*[516]

The competition for good gigs was stiff, and "the musical community of New Orleans underwent fundamental changes in this period, and the Creole-of-color musicians faced increased competition for employment, both from whites and non-Creole Blacks."[517]

Bolden played loud, probably too loud for the opera crowd, but the classical lovers weren't necessarily frequenting the Franklin Street clubs and tonks. Pops Foster said Buddy Bolden appealed to the "rough people" and played "blues and stink music, and he played it very loud."[518] Louis Armstrong, only six years old at the time of Bolden's top blowing, offered this remembrance of a gig he heard at the Funky Butt Hall:

> *Old Buddy Bolden blew so hard that I used to wonder if I would ever have enough lung power to fill one of those cornets. All in all, Buddy Bolden was a great musician, but I think he blew too hard. I will even go so far as to say that he did not blow correctly. Buddy Bolden had the biggest reputation, but even as a small kid I believed in finesse, even in music. In any case he finally went crazy. You can figure that out for yourself.*[519]

Who were these rough, unsophisticated people turned on by Bolden's blues? For sure the folks from Armstrong's back o' town neighborhood. And the folks who lived near the dump.

"In the heart of town, they had a big dump, and if you lived near it you sure could smell the rotten garbage and stuff. Later on, they started carrying the garbage out in the Gulf in big barges," Foster noted.[520]

Foster described another group of rough people:

We used to have backyard toilets in those days, and colored guys used to come around and clean them out. They'd put the crap in barrels, roll them out to the aggravatin' wagon, then haul them down to the docks and load them on boats, and they'd carry them off down the river. You could smell those aggravatin' wagons for a long way, and the only thing that would kill the smell was lime. The guys who worked the aggravatin' wagons made more money than any of the other colored, but most guys couldn't take it for more than a week. You could smell those guys coming—they smelled terrible. Those outdoor toilets caused some of the biggest roaches you ever saw. They were big red flying ones, and it really hurt when they bit you.[521]

The humanity, the insects, the sanitation, the humidity—in general, New Orleans was an urban pit, and Storyville was the back o' town.

"The mosquitos were terrible too. It was so bad in one place we played, named Howard's Canal, we had to wear nets over our heads," Foster said. "New Orleans in those days was a mess, very few streets had gravel, and only the ones like Canal Street had cobbles; most were just mud."[522]

In short, jazz was created by the "ratty people,"[523] said Isidore Barbarin, a grandfather of New Orleans jazz royalty. Brass multi-instrumentalist Barbarin was no slouch. He played with the Onward Brass Band, Excelsior Brass Band and Papa Celestin's Tuxedo Brass Band. Born in 1871, he was there when jazz was being created from ragtime and blues elements. Bolden, he said, "was famous with the ratty people."[524]

It's very likely Barbarin and Papa Tio heard the same bluesy work songs of the street peddlers. Louis Armstrong mentioned Lorenzo, a street peddler who eked out a living collecting rags, old clothes and bottles for resale. Louis said Lorenzo played "an old tin, long horn, which he used to blow without the mouthpiece, and he would actually play a tune on the darn thing. It was one of those long tin horns with a wooden mouthpiece which people used to buy to celebrate Christmas and New Year's."[525]

Would Papa Tio and Isidore Barbarin have dismissed Lorenzo's musicality, especially because of his low station? Very likely, but young Satchmo was enthralled. "When I was with him, I was in my element. The things he said about music held me spellbound, and he blew that old, beat-up tin horn with such warmth that I felt as though I was sitting with a good cornet player."[526]

Ultimately, Pops Foster came to realize that the audience often thought the musicians were too rough to associate with, especially out in the hinterlands.

Once I was playing Magnolia, Louisiana, and I was walking a local chick home after the dance. We were walking behind these two old hens and all they could talk about was those bad old musicians and what they did. It gave me fits. Musicians were nowhere in the South. If you'd play a dance in the country, you'd carry a few girls along to entertain at the dance. If any of the local guys would talk to the show girls, the local girls wouldn't have any more to do with them because they'd be out with those bad old show girls. Show people were classified as nothin' and musicians were rotten.[527]

Many early jazz musicians were not respected by their families. Jelly Roll Morton's grandmother feared his influence over his younger sisters, and when she realized he had been concealing his musical employment, she banished him in French, her first language. "Your mother is gone and can't help her little girls now. She left Amède and Mimi to their old grandmother to raise as good girls. A musician is nothing but a bum and a scalawag. I don't want you round your sisters. I reckon you better move."[528]

"Big Eye" Nelson described the emotional cost of playing jazz in the district. "Manuel Perez was one of the toughest cornets we ever had, a sight reader and a horse for work," he said. "Well, his people was very, very, very up to the minute, running back and forth to the church. A little bit this is a sin and a little bit of that is a sin—they'd have died if they'd heard of him being in the district."[529]

Bolden played at the Odd Fellows Hall in Algiers, a dance hall for Black people across the Mississippi River from the French Quarter. It was said the ratty people went there and the respectables to the Sacred Heart of Mary's Hall. The Odd Fellows had ham-kicking contests. The prize? A ham tied to a rope suspended from the ceiling for any woman who could kick her leg high enough to touch the ham, provided she was not wearing underwear.

George Baquet, a Creole clarinetist from downtown New Orleans, was surprised to see every man, including band members, wearing hats indoors. That was ill mannered and not something Baquet had seen in a dance hall before. Some band members lowered their suspenders and allowed their pants to droop. Bolden wore a hat and went tie-less, with the button of his shirt undone to expose his red flannel undershirt.[530]

"He'd have his shirt busted wide open. Every button open," noted Jelly Roll Morton. "And have a red flannel undershirt so the girls could see it and that was a great fad. They went and how did they go for those red undershirts."[531]

Throughout the nineteenth century, the music of New Orleans was dominated by Creole musicians trained in the European traditions.[532] The old-timers made a point of differentiation between the "players" and the "musicianers," and some of them felt that Bolden did not measure up. It hurt them to see relatively untrained musicians like Bolden get the fanfare and many of the jobs. The Creole musicians were a proud group, and it took them a while to accept the fact that their superior training and musical abilities were not putting them ahead of the Uptown bands that played lowdown "gutbucket" music (the gutbucket being the vessel used to collect chitlin-making hog offal). Others call it dirt music or ratty music.

New Orleans's insistence on segregation forced the music of its Black populace out into the open. The pride of Black people's ownership as Americans (conveniently ignored or forgotten by white folks) was an underlying force. Armstrong scholar Thomas Brothers noted that the New Orleans Black people who were essentially disenfranchised had little opportunity to be publicly Black, but funeral parades and subsequent second lines (the group of uninvited funeral guests on the street attracted by the funeral band following the procession) "offered…Negros a chance to assertively move their culture through the city's public spaces, the very spaces where African Americans were expected to confirm social inferiority by sitting in the rear of trolley cars and by stepping aside on sidewalks to allow whites to pass."[533]

Musicologist Charles Kinzer, in his writings about the Tio family, noted:

By the end of the first decade of the twentieth century a new kind of dance music, jazz had taken hold as the most popular style of the New Orleans music scene. Jazz had theretofore been developed primarily by relatively untrained, non-Creole black musicians, and with its characteristic elements of improvisation and driving rhythmic energy, it represents a highly Africanized approach to the materials of Western Music.[534]

Just as Armstrong's and Bechet's solo virtuosity evolved jazz past group improvisation, big band swing music was displaced by smaller combos, rock-and-roll displaced swing, the English wave supplanted rock-and-roll and rap pushed rhythm and blues to the side, Bolden's ratty jazz music forced the formally trained Creoles to play jazz or perish.

So, the fifty-one-year-old Papa Tio took a gig with the band of pianist Manuel Manetta around 1910 and by 1912 was playing a steady show at the Tuxedo Dance Hall, located at 225 North Franklin Street, a center of activity in Storyville. Franklin Street, like Basin Street, was so notorious that embarrassed city fathers changed its name to Crozat Street after the red-light district was shut down.[535] Personnel changed over the years as the band featured some of the prominent names of early jazz: Peter Bocage (violin), Oscar "Papa" Celestin (cornet), George Filhe (trombone), Louis Cotrell (drums) and others known to be "legitimate."[536]

On March 25, 1913, the *Times Picayune* reported the Tuxedo was "a model of the dance halls which make up a good part of the tenderloin."[537] The hall was about one hundred feet in length and thirty to forty feet wide, allowing plenty of room for dancers, a band, late-night revelers or slummers. At the "lower end was the band stand about twelve feet from the dance floor."[538]

"Here a negro band holds forth and, from about eight o'clock at night until four o'clock in the morning, plays varied rags, conspicuous for being the latest in popular music, interspersed with compositions by the musicians themselves," the newspaper said. The reporter misrepresented the bandleader "who grotesquely prompts the various pieces."[539] The writer was referring to a "comic entertainer,"[540] but the *Picayune* referred to him as the "leader of the band at the Tuxedo." According to Manetta, the band played out of the *Red Back Book*, which contained fifteen piano rags arranged for a small group. The combo also played "The Flowers that Bloom in the Spring" from Gilbert and Sullivan's *Mikado*.[541]

Like in the New Orleans of today, the drinking establishments were always competing for customers, and the proprietors of two rival dance halls, the Tuxedo and the 102 Ranch, engaged in a feud that might have signaled the beginning of the end of Storyville.[542]

A "New York hoodlum"[543] named Abraham Sapio, who changed his name to the less ethnic-sounding Harry Parker when he moved to New Orleans, and his brother, Isidore, who followed his lead and became Charles Parker, opened the 101 Ranch in 1910 on Franklin Street. The following year, the Parkers allowed popular New Orleans restaurateur Billy Philips to buy a piece of the bar. Philips bought out Harry Parker in 1912 and changed the name of the club to the 102 Ranch. Parker, in violation of his deal with Philips, turned around and opened the Tuxedo Dance Hall directly across the street from the 102 Ranch. The front of the new, larger, modern and better-appointed Tuxedo was wide open to the street.[544] Despite the Tuxedo's enticing sounds from Manetta's piano and Papa Tio's clarinet bleeding out into the street, Philips and his 102 Ranch consistently outdrew Parker's bar.[545]

Around 4:30 a.m. on March 23, 1913 (Easter morning), the waiters of the Tuxedo and 102 Ranch "brawled."[546] The *Picayune* was told the fight "was an old feud"[547] that occurred when the bars were supposedly closed.

> *The dance halls close up at midnight on Saturday and remain closed until Monday evening, when the saturnalias again begin....While there is no dancing or music after midnight Saturday until Monday night, yet the halls themselves cannot be said to be closed, for ranged along the wall on each side of the dancing floors are boxes or booths, in each of which is a table with benches for the accommodation of such as desire to watch the dancers while sipping beer, liquor or wines as the case may be, and here can always be found women and men in these boxes and booths even while there are no other attraction. Such was the case yesterday morning when the shooting occurred.*[548]

Waiters from the 102 Ranch went to the Tuxedo for a drink and got involved in a fight with the staff there. Parker threw out the inebriated 102 Ranch employees, roughing them up in the process while insulting the good name of Philips. The slur was promptly related to Billy. Billy, who previously had "several quarrels and one or two fist fights with Parker,"[549] went over to the Tuxedo, and after a short wrangle, matters seemed to simmer down. Billy returned to the 102 Ranch. Perhaps Billy should have left well enough alone, but it was the early morning of the Easter holiday. Did he have a genuine desire to be Christlike? He obviously emulated Jesus in the most unfortunate way. According to the *Picayune*'s "habitues of the underworld," Billy had "a view to ending the trouble and fixing up differences....[He] returned to the Tuxedo, taking with him two friends."[550] Billy put a dollar down on the Tuxedo bar in front of Harry Parker and "invited all hands to join him in a drink."[551]

It was then that Tuxedo waiter Charles Harrison, aka "Gyp the Blood,"[552] stepped up behind Billy and used a "method uncommon in the Crescent City but quite current in the northern metropolises of those years."[553] He shot Philips in the back.

The *Picayune* wrote that a shot "grazed Billy's neck," but another bullet must have hit home because Billy ran out and died on the curbside in front of his beloved 102 Ranch. The shooting was not over, as others were armed. Harry Parker ended up dead with a bullet in the back. His brother Charles was shot in the left arm, and assassin Gyp the Blood sustained a serious wound in the back of the head. Willie Henderson,[554] a young Black waiter,

The *New Orleans Times-Picayune* ran a full-page recap of the shootout at the 102 Ranch 101 years after the sensational brawl that resulted in the deaths of two popular and well-known saloon owners in the district. The violence closed the district dance hall for more than a year, sending the better jazz musicians off to Chicago. *From the* Times-Picayune, *New Orleans.*

was shot in the hand.[555] Curiously, Gyp the Blood survived his wound and two mistrials. There was no third trial, so Gyp got away with murder.[556]

What did it mean for Storyville? The police shut down the five dance halls in the district for more than a year. With no venues, many of the jazz musicians looked for other opportunities. The Tuxedo's band re-formed with trumpet king Freddie Keppard, clarinetist George Baquet, violinist James Palao and Bill Johnson on bass. They honed their style and set off for Chicago, becoming the first New Orleans jazz group to appear in the Windy City. Kid Ory and Mutt Carey also left town, as did the nucleus of the Original Dixieland Jazz Band.[557]

As for Louis "Papa" Tio, his days of playing jazz in nightclubs were over. There's nothing like a gunfight to dampen the enthusiasm of an older Creole gentleman whose 1812 ancestors served in Colonel Jackson's military band to play music to the wee hours in a dance hall saloon. He didn't give up music, but after the incident, he made his living solely as a cigar maker in a factory at 1726 North Villere Street in the Faubourg Marigny. The factory was owned by Ulysses Bigard, the uncle of Albany Leon "Barney" Bigard.[558]

Now that Papa had retired from the rough-and-tumble nightclubs, he had time to mentor Bigard's young nephew Barney. Barney got his finishing lessons later from Lorenzo Tio Jr., but Barney always remembered Papa and noted that "Papa Tio was a hell of a clarinetist."[559] Bigard went on to greater fame as a jazz clarinetist and was a member of Louis Armstrong's All Stars.

Murder, violence, prostitution, brawling, boozing, venereal disease— the city had enough outrageous fortune. Prodded by the United States Navy, it shut down Storyville. It didn't shut down prostitution, mind you; the business simply moved to other parts of the city. Jazz musicians still found work in the city, but when Louis Armstrong got the famous telegram from Joe "King" Oliver to go to Chicago, jazz left New Orleans. And New Orleans barely noticed.

The truth is, New Orleans was embarrassed by Storyville and ambivalent at best about its role as the birthplace of jazz. As early as 1890, before the music even had a name, it was denigrated by New Orleans society. Whatever the music was, in New Orleans it meant brawls, booze and brothels.

Al Rose in *Storyville, New Orleans* identified a racist and jazz negative cartoon in the *Mascot*, a weekly rag with a penchant for sensationalism, as the first illustration of a jazz band.

Several "coons" armed with pieces of brass have banded together….If their object was to inflict torture upon this suffering community…they are doing right well.... This man Robinson came here with a monkey and a blue parrot.... The town knew him not, but a n----r brass band betrayed him.... Robinson's balcony serenade is enough to make the dead rise.[560]

The Original Dixieland Jazz Band, a group of white musicians, recorded "Livery Stable Blues" in 1917, making it the first group to record jazz. This group of young men went on to tour the United States and England and were a sensation everywhere they went. The June 18, 1918 *Times-Picayune*, however, was beside itself in how to describe the music. Like a reluctant father denying paternity, the newspaper disavowed its creation. "It has been widely suggested that this particular form of musical vice had its birth in this city—that it came, in fact, from doubtful surrounding in our slums. We do not recognize the honor of parenthood," the less-than-proud father newspaper complained. "In polite society, and where it has crept in, we should make it a point of civic honor to suppress it. Its musical value is nil, and its possibilities of harm are great."[561]

The Black-owned *Louisiana Weekly* had a dubious opinion of jazz as well in 1926. "[Jazz] has its grasp upon the public so strong that it's a question of time when this menace will have to be checked by the law. [It] is breaking up more homes than the joy-riding automobiles,"[562] it reported.

Other state authorities piled on. The Louisiana Music Teachers Association noted at its 1921 convention at New Orleans's Grunewald Hotel that "orchestra and records that feature and deal in jazz will be lambasted in most unharmonious and unmusical fashion by the teachers."[563]

Jazz historian Charles Suhor found other negative references about jazz in the nation's newspapers. "Jazz was blamed for the heart attack of an elderly classical cornetist, an unfavorable trade balance between the United States and Hungary, the waning quality of Italian tenors, the frightening of bears in Siberia and the decline of modern civilization," he wrote in *Jazz in New Orleans*.[564]

It wasn't until 1932 that a New Orleans newspaper wrote something positive about jazz. E. Belfield Spriggins wrote a series of articles, "Excavating Local Jazz," for the *Louisiana Weekly*. Spriggins's writings reveal that he preferred a refined musical sound over jazz, but he acknowledged that Buddy Bolden's jazz and the musical venues of 1900 had cultural significance:

For quite some years now there has been an unusual amount of discussion concerning the popular form of music commonly called "jazz." The name followed the old name "rag time" which was more or less a modified form of jazz. Surprisingly, New Orleans has been either too modest to enter the discussion or entirely disinterested in the matter. New Orleans now speaks up to express itself. Many years ago jazz tunes in their original forms were heard in the Crescent City. Probably one of the earliest heard was one played by King Bolden's Band....The rendition of this number ("Thought I Heard Old Bolden Say") became an overnight sensation and the reputation of Bolden's band became a household word with the patrons of the Odd Fellows Hall, Lincoln and Johnson Parks, and several other popular dance halls around the city.[565]

But New Orleans did not take Spriggins's advice to promote jazz. Jazz scholar J. Mark Southern surmised that the city lost a golden opportunity when it failed to embrace jazz, the music created by the ratty people of the city.

In the first two decades of the twentieth century, New Orleans created a year-round tourist draw that reinforced the image of a wild spectacle commonly associated with the carnival season. Attracting jazz musicians as well as gamblers and prostitutes, Storyville solidified among tourists the perception of what New Orleans was supposed to be. Jazz figured prominently in that image.[566]

But even if the Storyville interests could have worked out a plan with the United States Navy, there were other forces that worked against New Orleans: Jim Crow and the Great Migration.

By 1945, New Orleans's Black population had declined, and the city had the smallest proportion of African Americans of any major southern city. Because of the population decline, the uniqueness of New Orleans Black culture was diminished and becoming diluted. New Orleans's war industry manufactured the famous D-Day Higgins boats that attracted a rural and southern Protestant workforce into a city long dominated by Roman Catholics. These *Americains* (a reference French-speaking Cajuns often use derisively to refer to outsiders) preferred hillbilly music, disliked jazz and were fearful of the permissive atmosphere in which it had flourished. Also, there were no Mardi Gras parades or riverboat excursions during the war years, so gig opportunities dwindled.[567]

While outsiders considered New Orleans to be the birthplace of jazz, there were few great jazz offspring to emerge from the city during this between-war period. By the end of World War II, "the city almost allowed one of its most recognizable cultural exports to die."[568]

These ubiquitous blue tiled signs are embedded in sidewalks throughout New Orleans and were the only reminders from 1921 to 1945 that Basin Street had ever existed. Said W.G. Zetzmann of the National Jazz Foundation at the 1945 name-changing ceremony, "Lots of jazz fans have come to New Orleans looking in vain for a street where the jazz bands played, Basin Street. They find instead, Saratoga Street. But if they look close, they find the blue sidewalk tiles here and there with the old name on it." *New Orleans Jazz Museum.*

In 1944, a Black Alabama schoolteacher named Sterling A. Brown traveled to New Orleans looking for jazz. He could not find it. He couldn't find the Kid Rena records recorded at New Orleans's own WWL studio and advertised by journalist Heywood Hale Broun in his New York–based *Hot Record Society Rag*. The record stores did not have it, had not heard of it and told him he could find it in New York. Sterling learned there were a few good jazz clubs in town, but he would not be allowed inside because of his skin color. He tried to visit the famous Basin Street of yore.[569]

"But I was not ready for its change of name to North Saratoga Street," Brown lamented. "After Canal and Rampart what New Orleans street could be more widely known than Basin?"[570]

All Brown got from his visit was "a sense that in New Orleans the feeling for jazz was nostalgic, commemorative, quite different from the force that sustained the young Louis Armstrong, Sidney Bechet, Jimmy Noone and Johnny Dodds."[571]

Jazz was not forgotten by the American public. It had flourished and evolved in Chicago, New York, Kansas City, Los Angeles and Europe, but New Orleans denied its role as the "birthplace of jazz" for nearly fifty years.

But jazz pilgrims were investigating the jazz cradle. Notable among them was musician, composer and researcher William Russell, who arrived in the Crescent City in the 1930s to collect material for *Jazzmen*, the first jazz history. He found a broken Bunk Johnson in New Iberia, helped him get dentures so he could play again and recorded him. Bunk's connection with the early jazz creators helped to herald in a new interest in traditional jazz and the city.[572]

Still, New Orleans resisted. There was great jazz to be found in the city, but it had disappeared in the areas frequented by tourists. The outrage of Storyville was gone, but the embarrassment remained. It was clear that prominent white New Orleanians did not see jazz as a potential tourist attraction and dismissed it as little more than suitable dance music. The reason for this embarrassment is as plain as the cultural divide between the elite and the ratty.

Historian Lawrence W. Levine wrote in *Jazz and American Culture* that old Eurocentric concepts of highbrow culture decidedly clashed with jazz. Levine suggested that in 150 years of the American experiment, no viable American culture recognized by European standards had ever been created.

"Who reads an American book? Who goes to an American play? Who paid any attention to American culture at all? Was there an American culture worth paying attention to?" asked Levine.[573]

Southerners may have been shocked when noted classical composer Antonin Dvorak suggested in 1893, "I am now satisfied that the future music of this country must be founded upon what are called the negro melodies. This must be the real foundation of any serious and original school of composition to be developed in the United States."[574]

The great marching band composer and conductor John Philip Sousa, for one, agreed with Dvorak. "Many an immortal tune has been born in the stable or the cotton field. 'Turkey in the Straw' is a magical melody; anyone should be proud of having written it but, for musical high-brows, I suppose the thing is déclassé. It came not from a European composer but an unknown negro minstrel."[575]

Consider the southern landscape of the first half of the twentieth century. The Ku Klux Klan was enjoying a resurgence in the 1920s. National politicians running for office had to publicly renounce the Klan.[576] In New Orleans, the concept of separate but equal was everywhere. A monument to General Robert E. Lee guarded the entrance to St. Charles Avenue, and monuments to the Confederacy were installed across Louisiana in the early twentieth century by Confederate apologists.

So it must have been shocking for the white New Orleans elite to comprehend that "Europe was coming to America for culture and the culture they came for was jazz."[577] Levine observed:

> *That this music which was characterized as vulgar at best and as harmful trash at worst by the Guardians of Culture and that for a long time was appreciated largely by those on the margins of American society; that this form of music which seemed so firmly ensconced on the American cultural periphery, should become the most widely identifiable and emulated symbol of American Culture through the world by the mid-20th century is one of the most arresting paradoxes of modern American history.*[578]

But some members of New Orleans's cultural elite did recognize that something positive was born out of the clashing and coalescence of so many varied cultural forces. Jazz was indeed born in Louisiana, and New Orleans was its cradle.

The mission to rename North Saratoga Street was the opening salvo in the cultural war with the New Orleans establishment to recognize that jazz, along with Mardi Gras, Sugar Bowl and the Vieux Carré, could be "a New Orleans gold mine."[579]

The National Jazz Foundation (NJF) was created in May 1944 as an "organization of people who recognize jazz as a musically and historically significant art form—and people who recognize New Orleans' historic connection with jazz as a potentially priceless civic asset."[580] Its name implied its reach was national, but it was composed of progressive and well-connected members of New Orleans elite society. Dr. Edmond Souchon was a prominent surgeon and a Pan American Life Insurance Company board member. Merlin "Scoop" Kennedy was a newspaperman for the *New Orleans Item*, and Myra Semmes Walmsley Menville's ancestral lineage included a Confederate senator, a Krewe of Rex king, a Boston Club (an exclusive club) president and a New Orleans mayor. They organized at Arnaud's Restaurant. Also present was Belgian jazz critic and writer Robert Goffin. Pat Speiss edited their mimeographed *Basin Street* newsletter. They had to be well connected to move the needle.

"At best, the Establishment [of 1940s New Orleans] maintained an attitude of malign neglect until the rest of the world made it totally clear that jazz—at least, some jazz—was okay," observed Charles Suhor in *Jazz in New Orleans*.

The NJF was telling the city, "Our jazz is good, something to be proud of."

No doubt high on their agenda was Basin Street. But before they could resurrect the name, they had to create a jazz buzz in the city, so they put on a show. Press releases went out, and the *New York Daily News* ran the item in its "Broadway" column: "The opening shot in the National Jazz Foundation's campaign to develop the history of jazz, immortalize its creators and foster contemporary exponents will be a two-day concert of swing by Benny Goodman at New Orleans' Municipal Auditorium Oct. 4 and 5."[581]

The choice of Goodman was solid but curious. Why bring in someone who had no tie to New Orleans? But the NJF also booked two local bands fronted by Irving Fazola (clarinet) and Sidney Desvigne (trumpet). Desvigne was a Storyville veteran and played on Fate Marable's steamboat bands.[582]

Buzz created, the National Jazz Foundation went to step two. On January 17, 1945, it teamed with *Esquire* magazine to produce the second annual *Esquire* Jazz Concert and brought in native son Louis Armstrong to perform at the Municipal Auditorium. The promoters set up three cities (New Orleans, New York City and Los Angeles) to host the shows.

The *Picayune*, not entirely sold on the "gold mine" of jazz, appeared to downplay the significance of the event and relegated it to a mundane "Amusements Calendar" article.

> *Louis Armstrong will sing Spencer Williams' famous "Basin Street Blues" at the Golden Anniversary Jazz concert at…the Municipal Auditorium. His rendition of the piece will follow a ceremony in which the name Basin Street will be restored to what is now known as North Saratoga Street. William G. Zetzmann, president of the New Orleans Association of Commerce, and Joseph P. Skelly, commissioner of public property in New Orleans, will officiate in the street name changing formalities. Armstrong, long noted for his jazz trumpet playing, and more recently for his jazz singing, is a native of New Orleans.*[583]

But the crowning moment of the event, at least for the National Jazz Foundation, was "giving back Basin Street its name."[584]

About midway through the broadcast, NJF president Scoop Kennedy took the mic and introduced chamber of commerce president William G. Zetzmann. "Lots of jazz fans have come to New Orleans looking in vain for a street where the jazz bands played, Basin Street," Zetzmann said. "They find instead, Saratoga Street. But if they looked close, they found the blue sidewalk tiles here and there with the old name on it. Today, on the occasion of this history-making concert, we're taking the faded blue tiles and putting them back where it belongs. Yes, we're changing the street signs and the city map."[585] The crowd shrieked with delight.

Back on the mic, Kennedy acknowledged Johnson as the "man who taught Louis to blow down the blues" before public property commissioner Joe Skelly interrupted with, "We're going to give the street back its name in proper fashion and we'll do it with our own worldwide famous tune. Let's have the Basin Street Blues!"[586]

And just like that, Basin Street was back.

In an epic journalistic fail, the *Picayune* buried the official name change under the inelegant headline "New Incinerator Planned by City" and reported the item with a blasé, "The council adopted an ordinance

FAMOUS BASIN STREET GIVEN BACK IT'S NAME—When the city of New Orleans changed the name of the famous Basin Street to Saratoga Street, letters from all over the nation began to pour in protesting the changing of the name of the world-famous thoroughfare. Wednesday night New Orleans officials gave the street back it's original name at a concert sponsored by the National Jazz Foundation. Left to right changing the signs are: W. G. Zetzmann; Joe Skelly; and Scoop Kennedy, president of National Jazz Foundation.
—NEA Telephoto

Once Storyville closed, the best New Orleans musicians migrated to Chicago and farther points. For twenty-four years, New Orleans denied its paternity as the "birthplace of jazz." The National Jazz Foundation, based in New Orleans, tried to sell the city on the marketing potential of jazz. It fell short but got the city council to "give Basin Street back its name" in 1945. This publicity photo circulated in several southern newspapers but surprisingly was not published in the *New Orleans Times-Picayune*. *From the* Sun Herald, *Biloxi, Mississippi*.

introduced by Commissioner Skelly changing the name of North Saratoga Street to Basin Street from Canal to St. Peter Streets. This was done at the request of the National Jazz Foundation."[587]

The *Baton Rouge Advocate*, however, allowed a jazzy write-up from UPI writer John Lewis Stone on the subject:

> *Although the Crescent City has been associated with Basin street for lo these many years, and even songs have been written about it, New Orleans has had no such street for about 20 years.*
>
> *But the National Jazz Foundation, which has secured a beachhead in the ranks of New Orleans hepcats, decided it was time something was done about such an incongruous situation.*
>
> *They marched on the City hall with a committee of solid senders and demanded restoration of old Basin street which was blotted out when the city fathers, in a fit of civic righteousness, changed the name to a more sedate North Saratoga street.*[588]

The National Jazz Foundation had lofty goals, but ultimately, it flopped. But as jazz historian Charles Suhor delightfully put it, it wasn't a *mere* flop.[589] It got Basin Street back on the map. The NJF acknowledged that jazz was a fully matured art form and a "potentially priceless civic asset." It helped tourists find jazz venues in the city, although sometimes tourists were unreasonable and wanted to know when the next jazz funeral would occur. The foundation published its *Basin Street* newsletter, held reunions for the old local jazz men and staged a Bunk Johnson concert for visiting French journalists, Jean-Paul Sartre among them. It sponsored a December 1945 high school jazz band contest that drew one thousand people to the Municipal Auditorium, teamed up with *Look* magazine and sponsored the southern regional of a national amateur big band/small combo competition, which was ultimately won by Al Belletto, an eighteen-year-old New Orleans home boy. It endorsed Bunk Johnson's 1946 Victor album (the liner notes listed an invitation to join the NJF) and financed his trip to a New York concert with Sidney Bechet. It hosted another big-name concert with guitarist Eddie Condon in 1946. It wanted to rescue Lulu White's whorehouse mansion, Mahogany Hall, and turn it into a jazz museum, but it was torn down in 1949 to create a parking lot.[590] (New Orleanians call this the "It ain't dere no more" phenomenon.)[591] The NJF got flashy publicity in *Esquire*, *Look*, *Newsweek*, *Down Beat* and *Metronome*, thanks to Kennedy and Spiess. The "Give Basin Street Back Its Name" photo appeared in numerous newspapers but, surprisingly, not in the *Picayune*.[592]

The 1970 New Orleans Jazz and Heritage Festival poster. Even though its traditional jazz heritage had become a major tourist attraction by the 1960s, New Orleans was slow to embrace its paternity as the birthplace of jazz, possibly because influential citizens still thought of jazz and Storyville prostitution as disgraceful and embarrassing. Segregation also played a role. Louis Armstrong often said he would not play New Orleans with his integrated band because the city's segregation laws forbade it, but those laws went away with the 1964 Civil Rights Act. The first International JazzFest was held in 1968, more than ten years after Newport, Rhode Island, began its jazz festival. The first official New Orleans Jazz and Heritage Festival was held in 1970, and it has become an enormous success. *New Orleans Public Library.*

By the end of 1946, it appears the financial support had run out, and the well-connected names did not sustain their interest. City trumpeter Johnny Wiggs hoped local bands would get more support but ultimately "learned that this fine group had no use for local musicians. They had to have big names like Benny Goodman, Condon and Louie. They spent thousands of dollars on these bands while the New Orleans musicians stayed buried under rocks."[593]

Then the high-powered Scoop Kennedy left to work for the Red Cross in 1945.[594]

Even so, the NJF name was attached to additional shows through 1948 that featured Armstrong and Stan Kenton. On the underbill was Stormy, a Bourbon Street stripper's jazz band. John Lester, a charter member of the NJF, was emcee and president of the NJF and romantically linked to the outrageous Stormy. Suhor suggests Lester got permission to use the NJF name to promote shows he produced, and it was rumored he ran off with Stormy and the proceeds from the big Kenton show.[595]

The final verdict from jazz historians? Despite the short-term big-time success of the National Jazz Foundation, jazz historian Bruce Raeburn thought the "NJF paved the way for the formation of the New Orleans Jazz Club." But Suhor felt "the NJF set land mines for any projazz organization that was unlucky enough to follow it."[596] Suhor added, "I cannot help thinking that the Lester and Stormy caper, whether true or not, is a great New Orleans story. It lends comedy, irony, titillation and absurdity to a great New Orleans story."[597]

One thing is for sure: the National Jazz Foundation gave Basin Street back its name. The Princeton, Indiana *Daily Clarion* put it nicely: "Well, there never was a song written about the North Saratoga street blues. People who went to New Orleans wanted to see Basin street and were disappointed when told there was no such place anymore."[598]

It's fitting that Spencer Williams waxed rhapsodic about a street that no longer existed because Williams was creating his own existence. Ultimately, he evolved into a significant composer of jazz standards and other pop songs. He claimed he was born on Basin Street to a prostitute mother. That's not true, but you know what?[599] It doesn't matter if you were born in Selma, Alabama, to former slaves (most likely but not startling, given the time) or birthed by a hooker in Storyville (exotic, but unlikely, also not startling given the time). When you're an African American helping to create a unique genre of American music during "separate but equal," you can create your own story. Don Draper (of TV's *Mad Men*; he stole his dead comrade's identity) and Clifford Irving (writer of a false 1972 Howard Hughes bio) told big whoppers (Irving got caught), but when jazzman Spencer Williams, the composer of "I Ain't Going to Give You None of This Jelly Roll," did it, it worked. I really want to believe he was born in a crib on Basin Street as Buddy Bolden jazzed up the blues at the club next door.

Williams did have a solid connection to Storyville, Basin Street, New Orleans and a house of ill repute. His auntie, the glamorous Lulu White, was a prominent businesswoman (okay, she was a prosperous prostitute) who built the Mahogany Hall on Basin Street in 1898. The ostentatious Mahogany Hall was the location of Williams's musical education between the years 1902 and 1907. He likely heard the jazz piano of Tony Jackson (composer of "Pretty Baby") and Albert Carrol and Buddy Bolden's trumpet.

By 1926, Spencer Williams already had several hit songs, including "Everybody Loves My Baby," for such jazz luminaries as Fats Waller. That tune was followed up with "I Found a New Baby," an even bigger hit. He wrote songs for New York music revues. He crossed paths with exotic dancer Josephine Baker in Paris and was well known in New Orleans, Chicago and New York. He had featured songs in the famous *Le Revue Negre* at the Paris Music Hall on the Champs-Élysées.[600]

The hits kept coming. "I Ain't Gonna Give Nobody None of This Jelly Roll" continues to be performed. His "Tishomingo Blues" was the theme song of the popular radio program *Prairie Home Companion*. He had hits from the 1910s through the 1980s, including the smash "I Ain't Got Nobody," which was a big seller for jazz man Louis Prima, disco legend Village People and rocker David Lee Roth of Van Halen under the title of "Just a Gigolo." What a life! He endured racism. He may have killed a man. He lived all over the world. His music endures and is played regularly by every trad jazz musician in New Orleans, New York, Toledo, Chicago, Tokyo and other cities. He died in Queens, New York, in 1965.[601]

If he didn't really grow up in New Orleans on Basin Street, and that's not the truth, well, it ought to be. Now that's jazz.

Chapter 6

TOOTS JOHNSON AND
OTHER UNSUNG MUSICIANS

Baton Rouge's best-known jazz musician was guitarist Mose "Toots" Johnson when Louis Armstrong first appeared in Louisiana's capital city in the 1910s. Johnson's is not a household jazz name, but as early as 1904, when jazz was being created, he was playing dances for LSU students. You could also catch him at riverside parks and social clubs.

On Armistice Day, November 11, 1918, from the "soldiers and sailors stationed in this city and also at the request of a large part of the younger set," Johnson was hired to perform at a large street party on Third Street between Florida and Laurel Streets to celebrate World War I's end.

Johnson is one of the unknowns described by jazz critic Ralph Berton. Berton said musicians like Toots Johnson were "certain good musician[s] of that time who did not have the chance to record [and who] will remain forever unknown."[602]

"Have you ever heard anyone talk about Frankie Quartell? He was the first trumpet player I ever heard use a glass as a mute," Berton wrote. "Do you know the name of Arnold Johnson, an excellent pianist of that time?"[603]

No, you haven't, and you've never heard of Toots Johnson either.

New Orleans is the birthplace of jazz, but in reality, jazz was born on the Mississippi River and bayou towns. New Orleans, Baton Rouge, LaPlace, Donaldsonville, Thibodaux, Abend, McCall, Parks, Opelousas, Crowley, New Iberia, wherever there were large concentrations of African Americans, the attitude was present and thousands of innovative musicians performed in obscurity for fun and profit. They fulfilled a needed role as great hometown musicians.

Midnight Frolic
For White People Only
Grand Theatre
133 Liberty Street
Tonight
Presenting Carter's
"Paramount Players"
Musical Comedy Company of 16 People
Direct From Chicago
Doors Open at 10:45 P. M.
Performance 11:30 P. M.
Admission (Including Tax)—$1.10
Tickets On Sale At

The Brunswick	Third Street
Wilson Music Co.	Third Street
Columbia Cafe No. 1	Third Street
Werlein's	Third Street
Columbia Cafe No. 2	North Street

Baton Rouge's Grand Theatre on Liberty Street was a venue for touring Black musicians and local ones as well. It often hosted performances by Black entertainers for white audiences. Liberty Street is now Baton Rouge's South Twelfth Street. *From the* State Times-Advocate, *Baton Rouge, Louisiana.*

When one considers that Bolden never played outside New Orleans, is it possible that he was responsible for creating jazz in rural areas? Jazz historian Austin Sonnier reported that New Orleans bandleaders like George Lewis, clarinetist Mutt Carey, clarinetist Buddy Petit and Bunk Johnson were mining rural parishes for musicians who "were concerned more with improvisations than with score reading," and they found plenty of good players. There were pockets of jazz in St. Martin, Iberia, Acadia and St. Landry Parishes, as well as Terrebonne and Ascension. Bolden, like Hypolite Potier and August Charles, acquired musical knowledge from slave parents and elders.[604] Before radio, jazz was spread by ear, by word of mouth, by train, by boat and by car.

Jazz critic Berton was talking about Louisiana musicians like Harold Potier (trumpet), Hypolite Charles (trumpet), Theophile Thibodeaux (trumpet), Lemon Ledet (bass) and Morris Dauphine (clarinet, alto saxophone) of Parks (St. Martin Parish); Mose "Toots" Johnson of Baton Rouge; Evan Thomas of Crowley (Acadia Parish); Gus Fontenette (trombone) and his daughter Mercedes Fontenette Potier (piano) of Iberia Parish; Lawrence Duhe (clarinet) of LaPlace (St. John the Baptist); and Claiborne Williams (cornet) of Donaldsonville (Ascension). All went undiscovered by the record-buying audience. Bands like the Banner Orchestra, Night Hawks and Lions Band of New Iberia; United Brass Band of Parks; the Joseph Oger Band, Black Eagle Band and Yelpin' Hounds of Crowley; the Vitale Band of Loreauville; and Martel Family Band of Opelousas—wherever there were sizable African American populations, the jazz was good. But their music was enjoyed only by folks who went to the fairs, halls, church functions and honky-tonks.

Musicians in the smaller towns didn't necessarily have to leave town to find gigs, especially if they already had a steady gig or a trade. Clarinetist Joe Darensbourg of Baton Rouge learned the cobbler trade from his father and could have had a career as a shoemaker. His family is still in the shoe repair business in Baton Rouge.

The Grand Theatre on Liberty Street was slated for preservation but is gone now. Ironically, when integration ended in Baton Rouge and the rest of the South, Black-owned business suffered and found it difficult to survive. The small theater business (Black and white owned) best served the public in the first half of the twentieth century. *Library of Congress.*

"The funny thing about New Orleans musicians," Darensbourg said, "none of them really wanted to leave. If it wasn't for the Storyville closing, none of those guys probably never would have left New Orleans."[605]

Though Austin Sonnier Jr.'s *Second Linin': Jazzmen of Southwest Louisiana, 1900–1961* is a slim volume, he does make an astute observation:

Geography, it seems, played a sizable role in the absence of recording activity. New Orleans where the bulk of music traffic was centered, was too far away and record producers were content with exploiting the talent there anyway. Nobody took much interest in going off to "discover" anyone after Bunk Johnson. Surely economic and social factors also played their part. So, the best years of Potier and some of Louisiana's finest musicians just went up in sound.[606]

Bunk Johnson, one of the top New Orleans trumpet players around 1915, did leave New Orleans, perhaps not by choice. Some suggest Bunk's reputation for drinking made him unreliable. He missed a Sidney Bechet gig because he was drunk, said trumpeter Lee Collins, who ended up with the job.

"He never liked New Orleans much to stay in and, in fact never liked to stay any place too long," said Frankie Duson. "He called New Orleans a 'dirty old hole.'"[607]

And even though Johnson often felt the caliber of the musicians surrounding him was inferior,[608] it was good enough in the hinterlands of south Louisiana and beyond.

Bunk was traumatized by witnessing the bandstand murder of Evan Thomas, which destroyed his horn, and by the time jazz researcher Bill Russell found him, he had lost his teeth. He eked out a living teaching music in New Iberia, working for Conrad Rice Mill, planting sugar cane and driving a cane truck to the mill during the sugar harvest.[609] His rediscovery by Russell "helped launch one of the most important aspects of the New Orleans [Jazz] Revival"[610] and played an important role in coaxing New Orleans's leaders to embrace their birthright as the cradle of jazz.

But looking for the other hidden gems in the musical mines of St. Martin, St. Landry, Iberia and Acadia Parishes? Those locales are 150 miles and more from New Orleans. And some were less, but anything outside the Crescent City was too far for jazz crusaders.

Baton Rouge, like New Orleans, had regular public music occurrences like the Firemen's, Labor Day,[611] Mardi Gras and funeral parades. "You heard a band on the average of two or three times a week, as small as [Baton Rouge] was," Darensbourg said. "They'd usually be advertising a dance or playing a funeral or something."[612]

Darensbourg reported, "If a cat [in Baton Rouge] amounted to anything or if he had any quality about him, he had a band playing at his funeral. You'd see those bands in any part of town. They had those lodges like the

Clarinetist Joe Darensbourg said funeral parades with brass bands along North Boulevard and Liberty Street were common among the Black population in Baton Rouge in the early part of the twentieth century. This one, for jazz great George Lewis in New Orleans, is from a more modern period but would have been fairly typical of any funeral parade. Darensbourg said he often heard "Nearer My God to Thee" played by a band of eight to ten pieces. Joe said, "If a cat amounted to anything or if he had any quality about him, he had a band playing at his funeral." *New Orleans Public Library*.

Odd Fellows that was affiliated with each other. If a prominent brother would cut out, they might have two marching bands for his funeral parades."[613]

The Sweet Olive Cemetery was a few blocks from the Darensbourg home, and the J.G. Winnfield Undertakers[614] was also close by, so young Joe had a good seat to experience the funereal music.[615]

"The only tune the funeral bands would play was 'Nearer My God to Thee,' with the drums beating 'boom, boom, boom.' Everybody marching, just like that, with the horses right along with them," Darensbourg said. "Needless to say, we kids would make a second line and follow the parade all the way. A lot of good musicians came from New Orleans to work in these jobs, like Buddy Petit and even Freddie Keppard. Those funeral bands would be eight or ten pieces, so they'd put somebody extra on there."[616]

Of the Baton Rouge bands, Darensbourg mentions three. "There was Toots Johnson's band, another led by a trombone player named Papa Augustin, and another by a tenor saxophone player name Tody Harris. Augustin was very good, but Tody didn't play a damn. He was a promoter really."[617]

Toots was also a promoter and bandleader and had a banjo player named Skeets do most of the rhythm work. "I thought Skeets was one of the greatest banjo players in the world," Darensbourg said. "I was crazy about the way Manuel Roque [clarinet] played and all those guys."[618]

Toots got most of the gigs. They were innovative and started using saxophones early. Toots, however, didn't read music.[619] And maybe he didn't have to since he had Skeets.

> *Toots used to work all the time. He had a lot of jobs and he played almost every night. He'd go down to New Orleans and hold his own, too. Toots could play with any of them. The other bands was only fair. They mostly played for dances and once in a while they'd get together and play for a funeral parade. But they wasn't in the class of Toots. Toots had a heckova clarinet player named Art Green. I know he couldn't read music. He was a real dark, heavy-set fellow, and I don't know where he came from, but I never heard a guy that play clarinet like him. I used to watch his fingers all the time. He'd pass in front of the house, and I'd say, "How come your finger ain't moving, clarinet player?" Ain't that a dumb question? Anyway, Green used to come to my dad's shop and get his shoes fixed. Sometimes he'd have his clarinet with him, and Papa would talk him into taking it out. And then he'd play it. And Papa would play his cornet and then I'd go get my clarinet and try to play right along with them. Green could play "Tiger Rag" and things like that like nobody's business. He was the one guy that made me say, "I'm really gonna learn to play that clarinet." He was the greatest of them all, in my eyes. Green played with Toots for a while and then Toots had another guy named Isidore Fritz who was very good. He was a bricklayer. A lot of these musicians was bricklayers and carpenters, trades like that.[620]*

Though Darensbourg didn't think too much of Tody Harris's playing, it was his first exposure to a saxophone and slap tonguing, a technique Joe became famous for with his big hit "Yellow Dog Blues" in 1957. Darensbourg's teacher, Manuel Roque, a regular in the Johnson band, played C-melody sax as well.

"The first saxophone I remember was this guy Tody, that played with Toots Johnson, slap tonguing on his damn tenor. I guess he thought that was the way it should be played. In fact, I fiddled around with a saxophone before, because my teacher Manuel Roque played C-melody back in Baton Rouge."[621]

How did the music from Baton Rouge and the small towns hold up against the bands of New Orleans? Just fine, thank you very much.

Eddie "Big Head" Johnson Sr., born in Baton Rouge in 1903, studied saxophone under Paul Barnes in New Orleans. As a twenty-something, he performed with such notables as Arnold Depass's Olympia Jazz Band, Oscar Celestin's Tuxedo Jazz Band and Arnold Metoyer. In the 1960s, he was leading his own band at the Harmony Inn with Alex Bigard on drums in New Orleans.[622] He heard all the greats and near greats.

"Well, during that time, jazz was really good," Big Head said. "Bands around Baton Rouge such as Professor Claiborne Williams and [Emile] Knox, and Toots Johnson's band, they were the only three bands at that time doing jazz in Baton Rouge."[623]

Guy Kelly of Scotlandville (a predominantly Black Baton Rouge suburb) played in Papa Celestin's Tuxedo Band but had some good-sounding bands in the capital city prior to 1927. The Toots Johnson Band also had Emile Knox and his mallet skill on drums and clarinetist Israel Gorman of Algiers.[624] Bands like the Banner Orchestra of New Iberia and Evan Thomas's Black Eagle Band also attracted top New Orleans musicians like George Lewis, Lawrence Duhe and Bunk Johnson for gigs, so it's safe to assume the small-town bands played jazz at a high level.[625]

Joe Darensbourg remembered Kelly's competing with a young Armstrong in the firemen's parade on North Boulevard around 1918.[626]

Darensbourg, who would later play with Armstrong, was the next clarinet player in a line of great reed players for Toots Johnson and began playing regular gigs with the Baton Rouge jazzman around 1920. That band included New Orleans legends Guy Kelly (trumpet) and Captain John Handy (alto saxophone). And after Guy Kelly left to go to Chicago, Buddy Petit, Kid Dimes and Kid Shots played trumpet with Toots.[627]

Pianist Eureal "Little Brother" Montgomery from the Florida Parishes town of Kentwood, who worked the Louisiana territory in the 1920s and later in Chicago, said that you didn't want to mess with Johnson's band, as "they'd blow away just about any other band."[628]

Darensbourg told of how Toots cut the LSU and Tulane University marching bands in one fell swoop:

I'll try to give you an idea of just how good Toots' band was. Whenever LSU played Tulane University, Tulane would bring their big marching band with them. They was the inter-sectional rivals. LSU would have theirs, too, and they'd have a big rally downtown. Somebody set up Toots' band this one time to advertise some kind of dance. When LSU got through playing, people would be there watching old Toots, and sometimes he'd break in there and just start playing. When he did that, the people would leave the LSU and Tulane bands just standing there playing and go over and listen to Toots. He had a one-eyed guy singing, using one of those big megaphones. He'd be singing up a breeze on "Sister Kate" or one of those tunes. When those guys were playing the blues, it sounded better to me than other bands. That's why I say black musicians was so supreme because they outplayed one hundred LSU musicians.[629]

And Toots welcomed cutting contests with New Orleans bands like Kid Ory's. "New Orleans is a big city, and its people would try to look down on us small-town guys, call us country folk," Darensbourg said. "When the top bands came, Toots would be ready for them."[630]

Darensbourg said Kid Ory's band would play at Bernard Hall at 133 Liberty Street (now South Twelfth Street).[631] Toots would be waiting next door at Bernard's Restaurant.

"While Ory's men were in the saloon, Toots figured to slip his wagon in there," he said. "They had a guy would lock the wheels. The idea was,

Kid Ory's LaPlace-based band in 1910. Ory, the great trombonist who wrote "Muskrat Ramble," would bring his band often to Baton Rouge in the 1910s to play at Bernard Hall on Liberty Street. His band and Toots Johnson's Baton Rouge band would sometimes get caught up in cutting contests—often won by Johnson. *New Orleans Jazz Museum.*

whoever you was playing against, if they figured they couldn't outplay you they would light out and run away, so when Ory came out he couldn't leave because them wheels was locked. All hell would break out."[632]

Toots had a trombonist named Old Tram who hated Ory. Ory hated Tram right back.

"Tram used to call Ory 'that goddamned yeller sonofabitch,'" said Joe.[633]

Included in this musical battle were Buddy Petit and Art Green with Toots, along with Tram and a club-footed piano player named Lawrence Martin and a fellow named Booster on the drums.

"Those guys could wail," Joe said.[634] "Ory had Ed Garland, Johnny Dodds, Baby Dodds and maybe King Oliver."

The results? "Toots run Ory's band out of town that day," Darensbourg said.[635]

It's entirely possible Ory told a different story in New Orleans. Darensbourg got to know Ory when he was a kid and later when he performed with Ory's band in California in the 1940s and '50s.[636]

"Ory was another one the musicians who used to come to Papa's shop [on North Boulevard] to get his shoes fixed. That's how I first came to know Ory," he said.[637]

Darensbourg also said Toots Johnson's promotional skills were as advanced as the times would allow. He promoted his dance, usually at Bernard Hall, by renting a horse-drawn flatbed furniture wagon, hanging advertising banners on the sides and ballyhooing about the town for an hour.[638]

"They'd stop in front of every saloon, play a tune, and the people would bring some beer out," Darensbourg said. "It was a regular Dixieland band, had a piano on it, tailgate trombone, everything. We kids followed those wagons all over Baton Rouge to listen to them play. I guess that was the beginning of the second line, although we didn't call it that at the time."[639]

The Johnson band wore uniforms, which was common. Johnson sat on the left; at his side was the clarinet. Sometimes, they would perform with two saxophones, and the trumpet and trombone would sit with the bass in the back line. If they could spread out, the reeds would sit on the end and the drums in the center.

For soft dynamics, Toots would holler out that he "wanted to hear the people's feet shuffling on the dance floor," Darensbourg said. "And when they'd get ready to close, you stomp off and hit it."[640]

The Toots Johnson band had opportunity to play dances at either the SPA Pavilion or Bernard Hall. Bernard Hall was open to the general public and was where sporting women and the "rougher element" went.[641]

"The bands did not change the music for either place. They played the same dance music, which they called ragtime and not jazz. Some of the old church people didn't like the music, wouldn't go to the dances and called the music evil."[642]

Toots Johnson was ubiquitous, and he is often mentioned as the entertainment of choice for social functions for Baton Rouge's Black community. His band was featured in Labor Day parades and patriotic parades frequently. He also participated in a Mardi Gras farce organized by the well-known local boxer Joe Daigre. Daigre owned a skating rink in nearby Plaquemine and often booked Toots Johnson for entertainment.[643]

On February 8, 1912, Daigre announced he would be "King of the Baton Rouge Carnival," but Toots rallied an insurgency and offered up his own petition for the kingship. Daigre was not going down without a fight and declared that since "he had organized the parade among the negroes that he is going to be king if he has to take it before the city council."[644]

The newspapers played along. In glaring racist fashion, the *New Advocate* quoted Daigre in Negro dialect: "Johnson ain't got a chance to be King. De people want's a king what got some quality to him. Den Johnson don't know nothing about being a King, while I have been educated in de King business."[645]

The parade was set to roll out. As Daigre's coronation neared, the band—probably the Johnson band—went on "strike."[646] "The tooter refused to toot and the drummer refused to drum," according to the *New Advocate*. Fortunately, "King Joe I [went] out on a diplomatic mission [and] a truce was arranged in time for the parade this evening."[647]

In 1913, the rival kings planned on ruling jointly over the Black Baton Rouge Carnival. The *New Advocate* again instigated a mock controversy when it noted:

> *There will be two kings, Toots Johnson and Joe Daigre, who have been rivals for the crown, will compete on Mardi Gras day. Joe came near having his title to the throne questioned by the police this week when he was arrested and placed in jail. It turned out to be just an ordinary fight at a dance. Joe managed to pay his fine and was released from the jail. The king is certain to appear unless another fight is pulled off.*[648]

In 1914, Toots had sole sovereignty over Baton Rouge's Carnival because Daigre was forced "to abdicate because of several disagreements with the police court."[649] But the white authorities had had enough of Black Mardi

A performer portrayed "Fiji Jim" in this circus parade in 1905 Baton Rouge. The costume might have been the inspiration for the outfit musician Toots Johnson wore in the 1913 Mardi Gras parade organized by him and Black boxer Joe Daigre. The Baton Rouge *State Times* noted that Toots was "rigged out as a Fiji Island chief…in the cannibalistic costume of the king, with nose rings, bells on his toes and a gleaming spear, tropical garb." Mayor Alex Grouchy might have been offended by the costume and denied future parade permits for the Black-organized parade by declaring, "A repetition of the annual King Dodo parade will not be tolerated." *Andrew D. Lytle Collection, LSU Libraries, Baton Rouge.*

Gras. On March 2, 1914, a week after Shrove Tuesday, the *State Times* sniffed, "A lot of good people in this city did not like the last one—received no inspiration from it, or anything of that kind, and felt more or less outraged at the whole performance."[650]

Toots may have pushed the limits of white sensibilities because he was "rigged out as a Fiji Island chief," which seems innocuous by today's standards, but "the cannibalistic costume of the king, with nose rings, bells on his toes and a gleaming spear, tropical garb, was a little too realistic to be approved."[651]

The aptly named Mayor Alex Grouchy was offended and declared:

The mostly mob which has appeared on the streets as a Mardi Gras celebration for the last few years has failed utterly to indicate improvement in any way, and offering neither instruction, amusement or redeeming feature.

Baton Rouge can well afford to dispense with such celebration of the day, and a repetition of the annual King Dodo parade will not be tolerated.[652]

The newspaper reported that Johnson was "too disheartened for words, crestfallen, defeated." The *State Times* did concede that he "had given the people of Baton Rouge an amusing, artistic and attractive parade," however.[653]

Black Mardi Gras was the only Carnival celebration in Baton Rouge and didn't return until the 1930s.[654] Mardi Gras was canceled for everyone in New Orleans in 1918 because of America's entry into World War I and also in 1919 because of the Spanish flu pandemic.[655]

Despite the Mardi Gras setback, Toots Johnson, the showman, promoter and jazz impresario, was ambitious and considered a western tour. George Murphy "Pops" Foster, from tiny McCall, Louisiana, a plantation community on the outskirts of Donaldsonville, considered going on the tour with the Toots Johnson band but balked when he considered North America's geography.

"In Baton Rouge, Louisiana, there was the Toots Johnson Band," Foster said. "It was very good and Guy Kelly played trumpet with them. They wanted me to go to Montana with them, but I found out it was very cold there and it was wintertime. I told them I wouldn't go because it was too cold, so they wrote a letter to find out. When they got the answer, they found out it was, so they didn't go either."[656]

To attract a musician the quality of Pops Foster, who played bass for the likes of Sidney Bechet, Duke Ellington, Earl Hines and Charlie Parker,[657] meant that the Toots Johnson band was a well-qualified outfit, even if they didn't exactly know Montana's location.

Gordon Lawrence, an LSU student who went on to seek his fortune in New York, was a fan of Toots Johnson. He was so enthralled with the jazzman's music that he composed "Toots Johnson," complete with the racist and sexist language of the day. News of Lawrence's publishing success reached the *State Times*, which enthusiastically stated the poem was published in the *New York Tribune*.[658]

One of the scribes got the facts wrong. Alas, Lawrence did not make the *Tribune* (it was published by the *Buffalo Evening News*).[659] Maybe to give Lawrence another poetry credential, the Baton Rouge paper also published his poem of lust and jazz.

The night grows old and lights dip low.
(Who can tell what a girl will say?)
If you don't ask her you'll never know.
Lips say "Stop!" but her eyes betray.
Press her a bit and then you may.
While Toots and his dusky fellows play
"Tiger Rag" and the "Beale Street Blues."
Caesar and clown return to clay?
True, dull Prince, to our sore dismay.
But bring no branches of mournful yews
When Toots and his band begin to play
"Tiger Rag" and "The Beale Street Blues."[660]

At the time of Louis Armstrong's first documented performance in Baton Rouge in 1921 as part of the Palmetto Jazzerites on board the *Capitol*, Toots Johnson was Baton Rouge's best-known jazz musician. There are no known photographs of Johnson, but there is homage to Armstrong in the form of a "Louisiana Legends" mural painted on the side of the Fletcher and Roy Building on Government Street just a few blocks from Liberty Street's Bernard Hall and Grand Theatre, venues where Black entertainers performed in Baton Rouge. *Author's collection.*

The beloved Johnson died at age fifty-four in 1928 of an apparent heart attack. The *State Times* ran a two-paragraph story of his death on page two:

> *Toots Johnson, 45-year-old negro whose dance orchestra has furnished music to dance-lovers in practically all sections of Louisiana and several neighboring states, and whose name to many was a synonym for jazz, is dead.*
>
> *Though he could not write his own name, nor read one musical note, Toots nearly twenty-five years ago began a two-piece orchestra, which in the course of time grew in size and came to be much in demand.*[661]

Notice of his death was picked up by the Associated Press and the Associated Negro Press. The obituary also appeared in the *Shreveport Journal*,[662] *Wichita Falls Record News*,[663] *Pittsburgh Courier*[664] and other small-town newspapers.

The Johnson reputation was so big that the band continued to perform under his banner until 1947. Years after his death, Johnson's name continued to receive high praise from jazz luminaries such as Joe Darensbourg and Zutty Singleton, people who knew what a good jazz band sounded like. Despite his local fame, there is no monument or historical marker today commemorating Toots Johnson in Baton Rouge.

In contrast, Louis Armstrong was a relative nobody when he made his first documented appearance in Baton Rouge in 1920 but became a star by 1928. There is a monument of sorts to Armstrong in Baton Rouge. His image is featured on a mural on the Fletcher and Roy office building on Government Street, about five blocks away from Johnson's home on Liberty Street. But Toots Johnson's story, formerly untold, is every bit as fascinating as Satchmo's.

Chapter 7

I THINK THAT LAST ONE
DONE ME IN

Murder on the bandstand, barroom shootouts, roadhouse gangsters, mental illness, police harassment—a traveling musician had a hazardous job. Notwithstanding the temptations of wine, women and avoiding jealous husbands and irate fathers, musicians endured difficult travel conditions, poor diet and bad dental hygiene.

Buddy Bolden "blowed his top"[665] in 1907 and died in the mental institution in Jackson, Louisiana. Joe Darensbourg said his shoemaker father did shoe repair for the institution, and he "always talked about the crazy musician up at the insane asylum."[666]

Henry Ragas and his bandmates in the Original Dixieland Jazz Band were "youths in New Orleans…in a street band that had been playing off and on since 1908." Despite being warned by Nick LaRocca's father, who said, "All musicians are bums," the band set the music world on fire with jazz and succeeded in New York. They were two days away from embarking for concert dates in Europe when tragedy struck.[667]

Pianist Ragas, "whose physical condition had been severely undermined by late hours and an excess of alcohol,"[668] had a "a few months of glory" but died in 1919 in the last wave of Spanish flu in New York.[669] His band members had stayed away from him for fear of getting ill themselves, but when it appeared the end was near, they visited Ragas daily despite the "vicious bulldog" he kept in his hotel room.[670]

Pianist Henry Ragas was a young man having the time of his life playing piano for the Original Dixieland Jazz Band, the band that recorded the first jazz record in 1917. At the height of the band's fame, just as they were leaving for a European tour, Ragas died in New York City of the Spanish flu, a worldwide pandemic that may have killed as many as 100 million people. *New Orleans Jazz Museum.*

Ragas died in the winter. Exposure to weather was a hazard to musicians, but singing about the weather could also have serious repercussions. Joe Darensbourg mentioned a ditty about rain in his *Jazz Odyssey*:

> *During this time "It Ain't Gonna Rain No More" was a heck of a popular tune. We used to have to play it about seven or eight times a night. By some coincidence they had a big drought in Louisiana. This was in the summertime, and it didn't rain for two or three months. The cotton was dying, so, being superstitious, the Louisiana people thought "It Ain't Gonna Rain No More" was causing the drought. Believe it or not, it was made illegal to play the tune. Several times musicians and bands got put in jail when they got caught playing that tune.*[671]

Darensbourg's account might be apocryphal, but the story made the rounds, as evidenced by this short that appeared in the *American Legion Weekly*:

George Lewis, born in 1900, was among the New Orleans old guard jazz musicians who went on to unexpected fame when he was rediscovered and recorded by jazz enthusiasts in the 1930s. He played music until he died at age sixty-eight in 1968. He has the unfortunate distinction of being on the same stage as two musicians who died onstage during a performance. *City Archives and Special Collections, New Orleans Public Library.*

No Wonder—The star comedian in the road show didn't know what had caused the riot in the theater until the day he left the hospital.

He had thoughtlessly sung "It Ain't Gonna Rain No More" in a Western town where a drought had prevailed for two months.[672]

But even just putting the horn to mouth could kill for wind musicians. Pops Foster related the tragic story of Thornton Blue, a New Orleans trumpet player out of the Irish Channel. Foster claimed he used to play with Blue's band around 1912–13.

"We mostly rehearsed and didn't have no job," Foster said. "I also worked with him driving cotton wagons for Grants. Blue used to play very loud and at a funeral one day he was blowin' so hard, he just dropped dead."[673]

Oddly enough, there is no other reference to Thornton Blue except for Foster's recollection.

But of all the musical demises, Papa John Joseph, one of Buddy "King" Bolden's musicians and neighbors, may have had the finest death any New Orleans jazz player could hope for.

Joseph, born in 1876, helped create jazz; *he was there*. He was part of Louisiana's Great Migration and relocated from Jamestown Landing in St. James Parish[674] to New Orleans. He led his own group in Storyville and played jobs with Claiborne Williams in Baton Rouge. Joseph played string bass, clarinet, saxophone and guitar with musicians like King Oliver, Kid Ory, violinist John Robichaux, cornetist Buddy Petit and violinist Pinchback Touro.

He came from a family of musicians and is the uncle of Don Vappie, a contemporary New Orleans–based banjo virtuoso.

When the district was shut down, Joseph settled into the barbering profession but remained musically active. He played bass on *The Chronological Smiley Lewis*, an R&B anthology that featured the New Orleans classics "I Hear You Knocking" and "Tee Nah Nah." In the 1950s, he played with Edward "Noon" Johnson, Lemon Nash and Punch Miller at the Associated Arts Gallery next to Pat O'Brien's. By 1961, the venue had evolved into Preservation Hall, a place where the older jazzmen could perform.[675] The Hall is still in operation today.

Concertgoers to Preservation Hall increase their likelihood of getting a request played with a cash tip, but a twenty-dollar minimum is required to hear "When the Saints Go Marching In." *Sam Irwin.*

String bassist Papa John Joseph on stage with George Lewis (clarinet), Dolly Adams (piano, back to the camera), Bob Matthews (drums) and Punch Miller (trumpet) at Preservation Hall. Miller, Lewis and Adams were all present when Papa John performed his last chorus of "When the Saints Go Marching In" on January 22, 1965. After a rousing version of "Saints," Papa John leaned over and said to Adams, "I think that last one done me in." Papa John then died on the bandstand. *City Archives and Special Collections, New Orleans Public Library.*

At age eighty-six, Joseph toured with Kid Sheik's Storyville Ramblers and recorded for Atlantic Records. In 1963, he toured Japan with clarinetist George Lewis. The band was wildly popular with the Japanese, and fans constantly sought to carry their luggage and Joseph's bass viol. The old musicians were in great demand in the United States as well, and Papa John played at the Baton Rouge Rotary Club's 1964 Christmas party.

By 1965, Preservation Hall was in full bloom, and Joseph was a "frequent and beloved"[676] performer there.

There is a rule at Preservation Hall. To request "When the Saints Go Marching In," one of the most popular tunes in the jazz repertoire, one must ante up a twenty-dollar tip. (It was five dollars in 1961.) Someone put up the cash because the Punch Miller–led band was playing it on January 22, 1965. When the final chorus was over, Joseph leaned over and said to pianist Dolly Adams, "That piece just about did me in."[677]

Papa John Joseph then collapsed and died on the bandstand.

Music moves us in many ways, and New Orleans, Louisiana, and the world are fortunate to have had Joseph in it.

Notes

Introduction

1. Conni Castille, "A Horse Tale from the Louisiana Prairie," *Attakapas Gazette* 4 (2014).
2. John Chase, *Louisiana Purchase: An American Story* (Gretna, LA: Pelican Publishing Company, 2002).
3. Angus Lind, "Song Satirist Benny Grunch Thinks His New Orleans Nostalgia Is More Relevant Now than Ever," NOLA.com, www.nola.com/entertainment_life/music/article_fedc5b3c-ca02-522c-afdc-3e1bee330343.html.
4. Thomas Fiehrer, "From Quadrille to Stomp: The Creole Origins of Jazz," *Popular Music* 10, no. 1 (1991): 21–38, www.jstor.org/stable/853007.
5. Gene Tomko, *Encyclopedia of Louisiana Musicians: Jazz, Blues, Cajun, Creole, Zydeco, Swamp Pop, Gospel* (Baton Rouge: Louisiana State University Press, 2020).
6. "The Melding of American Music," wyntonmarsalis.org/news/entry/the-melding-of-american-music.
7. Fiehrer, "From Quadrille to Stomp."
8. Ibid.
9. Ibid.
10. Ibid.
11. Donald M. Marquis, *In Search of Buddy Bolden: First Man of Jazz* (Baton Rouge: Louisiana State University Press, 1978).
12. Thomas David Brothers, *Louis Armstrong's New Orleans* (New York: W.W. Norton, 2006), archive.org/details/louisarmstrongsn00brot.

Chapter 1

13. Otto Fuchs, *Bill Haley: The Father of Rock 'n' Roll* (Gelnhausen, Germany: Wagner Verlag, GmbH, 2011).

14. NPR, "Louis Jordan: 'Jukebox King,'" NPR, March 4, 2008, www.npr.org/2008/03/04/87905064/louis-jordan-jukebox-king.

15. Wikipedia, "Your Rascal You," en.wikipedia.org/w/index.php?title=You_Rascal_You&oldid=999117675.

16. Ronald L.F. Davis, "Jim Crow Etiquette—September 2006," Ferris State University Jim Crow Museum of Racist Memorabilia, September 2006, www.ferris.edu/HTMLS/news/jimcrow/question/2006/september.htm.

17. "The Hit You Rascal You," n.d.

18. Tomko, "Evan Thomas," July 30, 2022.

19. Melanie Reiff, "Unexpected Activism: A Study of Louis Armstrong and Charles Mingus as Activists Using James Scott's Theory of Public Versus Hidden Transcripts," *University of Puget Sound Sound Ideas*, 2010, 35, soundideas.pugetsound.edu/cgi/viewcontent.cgi?article=1054&context=summer_research.

20. Joel Whitburn, *Joel Whitburn's Pop Memories, 1890–1954: The History of American Popular Music: Compiled from America's Popular Music Charts 1890–1954* (Menomonee Falls, WI: Record Research, 1986), archive.org/details/joelwpopmemories00whit.

21. Ricky Riccardi, "Six Minutes with Satch: When It's Sleepy Time/Down South/You Rascal You," Wonderful World of Louis Armstrong (blog), March 12, 2020, dippermouth.blogspot.com/2020/03/six-minutes-with-satch-when-its-sleepy.html.

22. Wikipedia, "Your Rascal You."

23. "Louis Armstrong: Rhapsody in Black and Blue (1932) | Early Music Video Starring Satchmo," 2019, www.youtube.com/watch?v=ThudMtzD3Io.

24. "The Permanence of Pops: Louis Armstrong and American Music," *PopMatters* (blog), February 3, 2013, www.popmatters.com/166813-the-permanance-of-pops-louis-armstrong-and-american-music-2495787704.html.

25. Reiff, "Unexpected Activism."

26. John McWhorter, "The Entertainer: Louis Armstrong's Underrated Legacy," *New Yorker*, December 7, 2009, www.newyorker.com/magazine/2009/12/14/the-entertainer-2.

27. "Louis Armstrong's 'Secret 9' Still a Secret," MLB.com, www.mlb.com/news/louis-armstrong-secret-nine-baseball-team.

28. Don DeMichael, Zilner T. Randolph oral history interview, February 13, 1977, rucore.libraries.rutgers.edu/rutgers-lib/66086/#citation-export.

29. McWhorter, "The Entertainer."

30. Louis Armstrong, *Swing That Music* (New York: Da Capo Press, 1993).

31. "Crowd Struggles to See Cornetist," *Times-Picayune*, June 7, 1931.

32. Armstrong, *Swing That Music*.

33. Laurence Bergreen, *Louis Armstrong: An Extravagant Life* (New York: Broadway Books, 1997).

34. Ricky Riccardi, *Heart Full of Rhythm: The Big Band Years of Louis Armstrong* (Oxford, UK: Oxford University Press, 2020).

35. F. Norman Vickers, "Dave Bartholomew, New Orleans Composer and Trumpet Player, Dies at 100," *The Syncopated Times*, syncopatedtimes.com/dave-bartholomew-dies-at-100/.

36. "Sensation," *Times-Picayune*, June 7, 1931.

37. Riccardi, *Heart Full of Rhythm*.

38. DeMichael, Zilner T. Randolph oral history interview.

39. Riccardi, *Heart Full of Rhythm*.

40. "Variety Will Be Offered Followers of Radio Dials in Programs for Tonight," *Times-Picayune*, June 18, 1931.

41. Charles L. Sanders, "Louis Armstrong: The Reluctant Millionaire," *Ebony*, November 1964.

42. Sarah A. Waits, "'Listen to the Wild Discord': Jazz in the *Chicago Defender* and the *Louisiana Weekly*, 1925–1929" (New Orleans, University of New Orleans, 2013).

43. "Louie Armstrong Had No Place to Toot Horn; Crowds Followed Him," *Pittsburgh Courier*, September 19, 1931.

44. Ibid.

45. "No One Wants to Talk about the Big Dance; Louis Armstrong House Museum Scrapbook 1987.8.5," *Louisiana Weekly*, September 20, 1931.

46. Robert Goffin, *Horn of Plenty: The Story of Louis Armstrong* (New York: Allen, Towne & Heath, Inc., 1947).

47. DeMichael, Zilner T. Randolph oral history interview.

48. Goffin, *Horn of Plenty*.

49. Bergreen, *Louis Armstrong*.

50. "DarkTown Stage Troupe to Face Judge Instead of Arkansas Audience," *Commercial Appeal*, October 7, 1931, www.newspapers.com/image/768620566.

51. Bergreen, *Louis Armstrong*.

52. DeMichael, Zilner T. Randolph oral history interview.

53. Max Jones, *Talking Jazz* (New York: Macmillan Press, 1987).

54. "DarkTown Stage Troupe to Face Judge Instead of Arkansas Audience."

55. Bergreen, *Louis Armstrong*.

56. Jones, *Talking Jazz*.

57. Bergreen, *Louis Armstrong*.

58. Jones, *Talking Jazz*.

59. Ibid.

60. "DarkTown Stage Troupe to Face Judge Instead of Arkansas Audience."

61. "Clerk Is Cleared in Sale of Pistol," *Commercial Appeal*, October 8, 1931.

62. Riccardi, "Six Minutes with Satch."

63. Janet Williams, "Cuckolds, Horns and Other Explanations," *BBC News*, July 4, 2009, news.bbc.co.uk/2/hi/europe/8133615.stm.

64. Joe Darensbourg and Peter Vacher, *Jazz Odyssey: The Autobiography of Joe Darensbourg* (Baton Rouge: Louisiana State University Press, 1988).

65. Ibid.

66. Ibid.

67. Ibid.

68. Austin Sonnier Jr., *Second Linin': Jazzmen of Southwest Louisiana, 1900–1960* (Lafayette: Center for Louisiana Studies, 1989).

69. Ibid.

70. Ibid.

71. Ibid.

72. Tomko, *Encyclopedia of Louisiana Musicians*.

73. Albert Valdman, "Ville (Ville)," in *Dictionary of Louisiana French: As Spoken in Cajun, Creole, and American Indian Communities* (Jackson: University Press of Mississippi, 2012).

74. Sonnier, *Second Linin'*.

75. Ibid.

76. Tomko, "Black Eagle Band," August 4, 2022.

77. Sonnier, *Second Linin'*.

78. Mike Hazeldine and Barry Martyn, *Bunk Johnson: Song of the Wanderer* (New Orleans: Jazzology Press, 2000).

79. Sonnier, *Second Linin'*.

80. Ibid.

81. William H. Gray Jr., "The Growth and Decline of Private Secondary Schools in Louisiana," *Journal of Negro Education* 8, no. 4 (1939): 694–701, doi.org/10.2307/2292911.

82. Sonnier, *Second Linin'*.

83. Gene Tomko, "Gene Tomko Talks about a Forgotten Jazz Great," *LSU Press* (blog), July 20, 2006, blog.lsupress.org/category/music/.

84. Ibid.

85. Sonnier, *Second Linin'*.

86. Ibid.

87. Thomas A. Sancton, "I Had to Make Music Like That, Too," *Harvard Crimson*, www.thecrimson.com/article/1969/5/21/i-had-to-make-music-like.

88. Tomko, "Gene Tomko Talks about a Forgotten Jazz Great."

89. "Dance Hall Is Scene of Killing Saturday Night," *Rayne Tribune*, November 27, 1931, acadia.advantage-preservation.com/viewer/?k=government&i=f&by=1931&bdd=1930&d=11271931-11271931&m=between&ord=k1&fn=rayne_tribune_usa_louisiana_rayne_19311127_english_1&df=1&dt=4.

90. Tomko, "Gene Tomko Talks about a Forgotten Jazz Great."

91. Darensbourg and Vacher, *Jazz Odyssey*.

92. Sonnier, *Second Linin'*.

93. Ibid.

94. Tomko, "Gene Tomko Talks about a Forgotten Jazz Great."

95. Sonnier, *Second Linin'*.

96. Ibid.

97. "Dance Hall Is Scene of Killing Saturday Night."

98. Sancton, "I Had to Make Music Like That, Too."

99. Sonnier, *Second Linin'*.

100. Tomko, "Gene Tomko Talks about a Forgotten Jazz Great."

101. "Dance Hall Is Scene of Killing Saturday Night."

102. Ibid.

103. Sonnier, *Second Linin'*.

104. Ibid.

105. Ibid.

106. Tomko, "Evan Thomas," July 30, 2022.

107. "Officer Ousse Kills Escaped Negro Convict," *Rayne Tribune*, September 4, 1936, acadia.advantage-preservation.com/viewer/?i=f&by=1936&bdd=1930&d=01311936-12311936&e=john%20guillory&m=between&ord=e1&fn=rayne_tribune_usa_louisiana_rayne_19360904_english_1&df=1&dt=2.

108. Ibid.

109. Ibid.

110. Sonnier, *Second Linin'*.

Chapter 2

111. Pops Foster and as told to Tom Stoppard, *Pops Foster: The Autobiography of a New Orleans Jazzman* (Berkeley: University of California Press, 1971).

112. Ibid.

113. "Quotes from 'O Brother, Where Art Thou?,'" IMDb, www.imdb.com/title/tt0190590/quotes.

114. "Steamer Capitol Has Wonderful Dance Orchestra," *State Times Advocate*, September 29, 1920, infoweb.newsbank.com/resources/doc/nb/image/v2%3A138FFE8785E79426%40EANX-13AE0503534B77BC%402422597-13ACB2E7519E6F42%402-13ACB2E7519E6F42%40?p=EANX.

115. "Joe Darensbourg Interviewed by Barry Martyn," RuCore: Rutgers University Repository, April 18, 1984, rucore.libraries.rutgers.edu/rutgers-lib/63477/JPEG/read/#page/1/mode/2up.

116. Anne Valdespino, "Saugus Dixieland Jam Honors Memory of Joe Darensbourg," *Los Angeles Times*, June 10, 1985, www.latimes.com/archives/la-xpm-1985-06-10-me-5931-story.html.

117. "All US Top 40 Singles for 1958," Top40Weekly.Com, November 30, 2013, top40weekly.com/1958-all-charts.

118. "'It's Awful Nice to Be Up There Among All Them Beatles': The Story of 'Hello, Dolly!,'" That's My Home, December 3, 2021, virtualexhibits. louisarmstronghouse.org/2021/12/03/its-awful-nice-to-be-up-there-among-all-them-beatles-the-story-of-hello-dolly.

119. Darensbourg and Vacher, *Jazz Odyssey*.

120. Ibid.

121. Ibid.

122. Ibid.

123. Ibid.

124. Ibid.

125. Ibid.

126. Ibid.

127. Ibid.

128. Ibid.

129. Ibid.

130. Ibid.

131. Ibid.

132. Ibid.

133. Ibid.

134. "Dance at Chataignier," *Weekly Gazette*, February 16, 1924, www.newspapers. com/image/474298894/?terms=%22Martel%20Band%22&match=1.

135. Ibid.

136. "Parker Declares War Upon K.K.K.," *Weekly Gazette*, April 22, 1922, sec. 1, www.newspapers.com/image/478398888/?terms=%22Ku%20Klux%20Klan%22&match=1.

137. Earl Rovit, "The Twenties," *The Sewanee Review* 122, no. 1 (2014): 115–23, www.jstor.org/stable/43662793.

138. Darensbourg and Vacher, *Jazz Odyssey*.

139. Ibid.

140. Ibid.

141. Little Old Man, "Euzebe Vidrine Pays Price for Murder," *Weekly Gazette*, August 9, 1924, www.newspapers.com/image/474309174/?terms=%22Euzebe%20Vidrine%22&match=1.

142. "Waylay, Shoot and Mortally Wounds Evangeline Farmer," *St. Landry Clarion*, April 30, 1921.

143. Ibid.

144. "Slew White Man in Allen Parish and Caught Here," *St. Landry Clarion*, April 30, 1921.

145. "Evangeline Man Takes Own Life," *St. Landry Clarion*, April 30, 1921.

146. "Two White Men Fight, Both Die," *St. Landry Clarion*, April 30, 1921.

147. "Episode 79 Serial Killer Euzebe Vidrine," Southern Mysteries, January 11, 2021, southernmysteries.com/2021/01/11/serialkillereuzebevidrine.

148. Carola Lillie Hartley, "Euzebe Vidrine and the Murder of Robert Leo Wiggins | Parlons Opelousas," *Daily World*, July 10, 2021, www.dailyworld.com/story/news/local/2021/07/10/euzebe-vidrine-and-murder-robert-leo-wiggins-parlons-opelousas/7913249002.

149. "Waylay, Shoot and Mortally Wounds Evangeline Farmer."

150. Euzebe Vidrine, *The Life of Euzebe Vidrine* (Opelousas, LA: Clarion Co., 1924).

151. "Succumbs to Wounds," *Weekly Gazette*, May 7, 1921, www.newspapers.com/clip/33453146/the-ville-platte-gazette.

152. Vidrine, *Life of Euzebe Vidrine*.

153. Ibid.

154. "Grand Jury Report," *Weekly Gazette*, May 28, 1921, www.newspapers.com/image/478402582/?terms=%22Euzebe%20Vidrine%22&match=1.

155. "Criminal Court in Session," *Ville Platte Gazette*, June 25, 1921, www.newspapers.com/image/478403005/?terms=%22Euzebe%20Vidrine%22&match=1.

156. Vidrine, *Life of Euzebe Vidrine*.

157. "Episode 79 Serial Killer Euzebe Vidrine."

158. Vidrine, *Life of Euzebe Vidrine*.

159. Ibid.

160. Ibid.

161. Ibid.

162. Ibid.

163. Ibid.

164. "Crowley Has Mysterious Murder Also," *Daily Advertiser*, December 2, 1921.

165. "Jitney Driver Is Found Dead on Road," *Galveston Daily News*, December 14, 1921, sec. 1.

166. Vidrine, *Life of Euzebe Vidrine*.

167. "Orange Court Has Big Criminal Docket," *Houston Post*, April 24, 1922.

168. "Convicted Slayer of Duke Denied New Trial," *Houston Post*, May 28, 1922.

169. Ruby Maloni, "Dissonance Between Norms and Behaviour: Early 20th Century America's New Woman," *Proceedings of the Indian History Congress* 70 (2009): 880–86, www.jstor.org/stable/44147735.

170. "Sheriff's Sale," *Weekly Gazetteer*, April 1, 1922, www.newspapers.com/image/478398110/?terms=%22Euzebe%20Vidrine%22&match=1.

171. Ted Hinton and as told to Larry Grove, *Ambush: The Real Story of Bonnie and Clyde* (Dallas: Ken M. Holmes Jr., 1979).

172. Vidrine, *Life of Euzebe Vidrine*.

173. Ibid.

174. Ibid.

175. "Cold Blooded Assassination," *Weekly Gazette*, May 24, 1924.

176. Ibid.

177. Ibid.

178. Vidrine, *Life of Euzebe Vidrine*.

179. Ibid.

180. "Leo Wiggins Is Murdered Near Ville Platte by Man Dazed with Moonshine," *St. Landry Clarion*, May 24, 1924.

181. "Cold Blooded Assassination."

182. Vidrine, *Life of Euzebe Vidrine*.

183 "Leo Wiggins Is Murdered Near Ville Platte by Man Dazed with Moonshine."

184. "Cold Blooded Assassination."

185. "Leo Wiggins Is Murdered Near Ville Platte by Man Dazed with Moonshine."

186. Vidrine, *Life of Euzebe Vidrine*.

187. "Welcome Callers," *Weekly Gazette*, August 9, 1924.

188. "Makes His Hanging Lesson to Community; Louisiana Murderer Is Photographed, Makes a Speech and Has His Coffin Put on View," *New York Times*, August 9, 1924, sec. Archives, www.nytimes.com/1924/08/09/archives/makes-his-hanging-lesson-to-community-louisiana-murderer-is.html.

189. "Miscellany: Aug. 18, 1924," *Time*, August 18, 1924, content.time.com/time/subscriber/article/0,33009,718977,00.html.

190. Ibid.

191. Little Old Man, "Euzebe Vidrine Pays Price for Murder," *Weekly Gazette* (Ville Platte, LA), August 9, 1924, www.newspapers.com/image/474309174/?terms=%22Euzebe%20Vidrine%22&match=1.

192. United Press, "Vidrine Hangs Today, Killed Louisiana Man," *Imperial Valley Press*, August 8, 1924.

193. "Texan Is in Prison for Murder Vidrine Says He Committed," *Shreveport Journal*, August 8, 1924, www.newspapers.com/image/600077963/.

194. Vidrine, *Life of Euzebe Vidrine*.

195. "A Copy of The Life of Euzebe Vidrine," *Daily Advertiser*, July 24, 1924.

196. "The 'Moral Effect' of 'Vidrine's Life of Crime,'" *Weekly Gazette*, August 9, 1924.

197. Vidrine, *Life of Euzebe Vidrine*.

198. "Services Held in Cell of Slayer Doomed to Hang," *Shreveport Journal*, July 28, 1924.

199. "Request His Body Put on Exhibition Following Hanging," *Buffalo Courier*, August 9, 1924.

200. Darensbourg and Vacher, *Jazz Odyssey*.

201. Shane K. Bernard, *The Cajuns: Americanization of a People* (Jackson: University Press of Mississippi, 2003).

202. Maloni, "Dissonance Between Norms and Behaviour."

203. Rovit, "The Twenties."

204. "Probe of Slaying Is Conducted Upon Chicago U. Campus," *Daily Advertiser*, May 30, 1924.

205. "Cold Blooded Assassination."

206. "Services Held in Cell of Slayer Doomed to Hang."

207. "Euzebe Vidrine," *Weekly Gazette*, August 9, 1924.

208. Darensbourg and Vacher, *Jazz Odyssey*.

209. Ibid.

210. Ibid.

211. Ibid.

212. Ibid.

213. Ibid.

214. Ibid.

215. "Advertisement—BostonElectric Shoe Shop; I. Chapman, Proprietor," *St. Landry Clarion*, February 28, 1920.

216. Darensbourg and Vacher, *Jazz Odyssey*.

217. Ibid.

218. Ibid.

219. Ibid.

220. "Moon Medicine Show," *Weekly Iberian*, February 10, 1927.

221. Darensbourg and Vacher, *Jazz Odyssey*.

222. Ibid.

223. Gary DeNeal, *A Knight of Another Sort: Prohibition Days and Charlie Birger*, 2nd ed. (Carbondale: Southern Illinois University Press, 1998).

224. "Little Egypt in the 19th Century," Little Egypt in the Civil War, littleegyptcivilwar. leadr.msu.edu/understanding-egypt-introduction/understanding-egypt-geography-and-name.; United Press, "Drouth Parches 'Little Egypt,'" *Marion Evening Post*, July 2, 1926.

225. DeNeal, *Knight of Another Sort*.

226. Foster and as told to Tom Stoppard, *Pops Foster*.

227. DeNeal, *Knight of Another Sort*.

228. "S. Glen Young Weds Two Weeks After Divorce," *Belleville News-Democrat*, July 18, 1921.

229. E. Bishop Hill, *Complete History of Southern Illinois' Gang War* (self-published, 1927; repr., London: Forgotten Books, 2018), 102.

230. DeNeal, *Knight of Another Sort*.

231. Ibid.

232. Ibid.

233. "Decisions at Danville Not for Bootlegger," *Daily Independent*, March 14, 1924.

234. United Press, "Glen Young Indicted," *De Kalb Daily Chronicle*, February 14, 1924.
235. "Raids Not to Stop—Young: Ministers and Klan Say Placing Troops in Williamson Big Farce," *Carbondale Free Press*, January 9, 1924.
236. Ibid.
237. Ibid.
238. DeNeal, *Knight of Another Sort*.
239. "99 Indictments by Herrin Jury," *Moline Daily Dispatch*, March 14, 1924.
240. DeNeal, *Knight of Another Sort*.
241. "Murders Feature Clash Between Klan and Anti-Klan in Liquor Raids," *Edwardsville Intelligencer*, February 9, 1924.
242. Ibid.
243. "99 Indictments by Herrin Jury."
244. DeNeal, *Knight of Another Sort*.
245. "99 Indictments by Herrin Jury."
246. DeNeal, *Knight of Another Sort*.
247. Hill, "Complete History of Southern Illinois' Gang War."
248. Ibid.
249. DeNeal, *Knight of Another Sort*.
250. Darensbourg and Vacher, *Jazz Odyssey*.
251. Ibid.
252. Ibid.
253. Ibid.
254. Ibid.
255. Anonymous, *Life and Exploits of S. Glenn Young: World-Famous Law Enforcement Officer* (Mrs. S. Glenn Young, 1924), libsysdigi.library.illinois.edu/oca/Books2008-08/lifeexploitsofsg00herr/lifeexploitsofsg00herr.pdf.
256. Ibid.
257. Ibid.
258. Darensbourg and Vacher, *Jazz Odyssey*.
259. "Williamson Co. Described as a Bit of Hell," *Daily Advocate*, January 11, 1924.
260. Bergreen, *Louis Armstrong*.
261. "Williamson Co. Described as a Bit of Hell."
262. "France Roused by Dry Terror in Williamson," *Chicago Daily Tribune*, February 8, 1924.
263. Charles A. Sengstock Jr., "Roadhouses," Encyclopedia of Chicago, 2005, www.encyclopedia.chicagohistory.org/pages/1082.html.
264. Hill, "Complete History of Southern Illinois' Gang War."
265. Ibid.
266. "Eddie Miller Broadcast," *Marion Evening Post*, January 24, 1925.
267. Darensbourg and Vacher, *Jazz Odyssey*.
268. "Eddie Miller Broadcast."

269. Darensbourg and Vacher, *Jazz Odyssey*.

270. DeNeal, *Knight of Another Sort*.

271. Ibid.

272. "All US Top 40 Singles for 1958," Top40Weekly.Com.

273. Darensbourg and Vacher, *Jazz Odyssey*.

274. Valdespino, "Saugus Dixieland Jam Honors Memory of Joe Darensbourg."

275. DeNeal, *Knight of Another Sort*.

276. Ibid.

277. Hill, "Complete History of Southern Illinois' Gang War."

278. Darensbourg and Vacher, *Jazz Odyssey*.

279. Ibid.

280. Ibid.

281. Ibid.

282. Ibid.

283. DeNeal, *Knight of Another Sort*.

284. Ibid.

285. Fred J. Kern, "Ku Klux Klan Is Dead and Long May the Old Brute Beast Stay Dead," *Belleville News-Democrat*, July 10, 1926.

286. "Two Men Killed in Roadhouse Argument Near Marion Monday," *Marion Evening Post*, August 23, 1926.

287. "Former C'Dale Girl Testifies in Herrin Killing," *Carbondale Free Press*, July 15, 1926.

288. DeNeal, *Knight of Another Sort*.

289. "More Trouble Expected at Herrin Today," *Clinton Daily Public*, July 7, 1926.

290. "New Confession in Connection with Mail Man Murder," *Daily Advocate*, August 11, 1926.

291. United Press, "Saline County after Reputation of Williamson," *Marion Evening Post*, August 16, 1926.

292. "Marion Post Predicts War in Coal Belt," *Daily Independent*, August 24, 1926.

293. Ibid.

294. Darensbourg and Vacher, *Jazz Odyssey*.

295. "Rifles, Pistols Are Seized in Large Quantity," *Carbondale Free Press*, August 27, 1926.

296. Darensbourg and Vacher, *Jazz Odyssey*.

297. Ibid.

298. Ibid.

299. "Marion Post Predicts War in Coal Belt."

300. Darensbourg and Vacher, *Jazz Odyssey*.

301. Ibid.

302. "Joe Darensbourg Interviewed by Barry Martyn."

303. DeNeal, *Knight of Another Sort*.

304. Ibid.

305. "Booze, Blood and Bombs: Prohibition in Southern Illinois," NPR Illinois, August 13, 2020, www.nprillinois.org/illinois/2020-08-13/booze-blood-and-bombs-prohibition-in-southern-illinois.

306. DeNeal, *Knight of Another Sort.*

Chapter 3

307. Louis Armstrong, *Satchmo: My Life in New Orleans* (New York: Da Capo Press, 1954).

308. "Louis Armstrong House Museum," Louis Armstrong Home Museum, www.louisarmstronghouse.org/books.

309. Richard Havers, "Louis Armstrong's Birthday: A Jazz Mystery," *UDiscover Music* (blog), August 4, 2021, www.udiscovermusic.com/stories/louis-armstrongs-birthday/.

310. Ricky Riccardi, "Happy Birthday, Pops! (The Case for July 4, 1901…)," *The Wonderful World of Louis Armstrong* (blog), dippermouth.blogspot.com/2015/07/happy-birthday-pops-case-for-july-4-1901.html.

311. "Reel-to-Reel Tape Recorded by Louis Armstrong—LAHM Tape 425/Louis Tape 123—Track 2," digital recording (Queens, New York, 1970), collections.louisarmstronghouse.org/asset-detail/1160450.

312. "14 of the Best Protest Songs of the '60s and '70s," LiveAbout, www.liveabout.com/anti-war-protest-songs-of-the-60s-and-70s-748278.

313. "Reel-to-Reel Tape Recorded by Louis Armstrong."

314. Riccardi, "Happy Birthday, Pops!"

315. "Reidel's Slayers Both Indicted. Promptness of Trial Will Depend. Upon Allotment, One Section of Court," *Times-Picayune*, October 22, 1910, infoweb.newsbank.com/apps/news/openurl?ctx_ver=z39.88-2004&rft_id=info%3Asid/infoweb.newsbank.com&svc_dat=AMNEWS&req_dat=1006417D79E1C198&rft_val_format=info%3Aofi/fmt%3Akev%3Amtx%3Actx&rft_dat=document_id%3Aimage%252Fv2%253A1223BCE5B718A166%2540EANX-122931A148CA1F40%25402418967-12282662525C8408%25403-1275ABD3482F312C%2540Reidel%252527s%252BSlayers%252BBoth%252BIndicted.%252BPromptness%252Bof%252BTrial%252BWill%252BDepend.%252BUpon%252BAllotment%25252C%252BOne%252BSection%252Bof%252BCourt/hlterms%3A%2522Louis%2520Armstrong%2522%2520%25221910%2522.

316. Ibid.

317. Staff of the *Times-Democrat*, "New Orleans *Times-Democrat* newspaper Item, 2 January 1913. Noting Arrests at New Year Celebrations, Including Young Louis Armstrong. (Armstrong Was Sentenced to Time in the 'Colored Waif's Home,' Where He Learned Trumpet)," January 2, 1913, commons.wikimedia.org/wiki/File:Louis_Armstrong_Arrest_2_Jan_1913_Times-Democrat.jpg.

318. Riccardi, "Happy Birthday, Pops!"

319. Bruce Eggler, "Armstrong: Give or Take a Year," *Times-Picayune*, September 24, 1988, sec. B, infoweb.newsbank.com/apps/news/document-view?p=AMNEWS&t=pubname%3A1223BCE5B718A166%21Times-Picayune&sort=YMD_date%3AA&page=1&fld-nav-0=YMD_date&val-nav-0=1970%20-%201990&fld-base-0=alltext&maxresults=20&val-base-0=%22Tad%20Jones%22&docref=image/v2%3A1223BCE5B718A166%40EANX-1341E293BAE80F05%402447429-1340E2B50F62350A%4012-1340E2B50F62350A%40.

320. Ibid.

321. "Happy Unbirthday, Satchmo," *Times-Picayune*, July 4, 1989, sec. C, infoweb.newsbank.com/apps/news/document-view?p=AMNEWS&t=pubname%3A1223BCE5B718A166%21Times-Picayune&sort=YMD_date%3AA&page=1&fld-nav-0=YMD_date&val-nav-0=1970%20-%201990&fld-base-0=alltext&maxresults=20&val-base-0=%22Tad%20Jones%22&docref=image/v2%3A1223BCE5B718A166%40EANX-16A399DAE43BDC1E%402447712-16A2F907C7445368%4048-16A2F907C7445368%40.

322. Bergreen, *Louis Armstrong*.

323. "'What to the Slave Is the Fourth of July?': The History of Frederick Douglass' Searing Independence Day Oration," *Time*, time.com/5614930/frederick-douglass-fourth-of-july.

324. Sam Irwin, Kathee Hambrick interview, January 25, 2022.

325. "Declaration of Independence: A Transcription," National Archives, November 1, 2015, www.archives.gov/founding-docs/declaration-transcript.

326. "What to the Slave Is the Fourth of July?"

327. "Randy Newman: Good Old Boys: Music Reviews: Rolling Stone," June 10, 2008, web.archive.org/web/20080610173539, www.rollingstone.com/artists/randynewman/albums/album/129751/review/6068141/good_old_boys.

328. Armstrong, *Satchmo*.

329. Bergreen, *Louis Armstrong*.

330. "Louisiana Reconstructed, 1863–1877" (Louisiana State University Press, 1974).

331. BlackPast, "What, to the Slave, Is the Fourth of July?," January 25, 2007, www.blackpast.org/african-american-history/speeches-african-american-history/1852-frederick-douglass-what-slave-fourth-july.

332. Ethan J. Kytle Roberts Blain, "When the Fourth of July Was a Black Holiday," *Atlantic*, July 3, 2018, www.theatlantic.com/ideas/archive/2018/07/fourth-of-july-black-holiday/564320/.

333. Ibid.

334. "Louisiana Reconstructed, 1863–1877."

335. "The Fourth Passed Quietly Away," *Tri-Weekly Advocate*, July 5, 1867, infoweb.newsbank.com/apps/news/document-view?p=AMNEWS

&t=pubname%3A138FFECC909AB153%21Daily%2BAdvocate/
year%3A1867%211867/mody%3A0705%21July%2B05&action=browse&
year=1867&format=image&docref=image%2Fv2%3A138FFECC909AB
153%40EANX-13A3CC82D7B5AB01%402403153-13A376E7C9E6FC4
4%401&origin=image%2Fv2%3A138FFECC909AB153%40EANX-
13A3CC82D7B5AB01%402403153-13A376E7C479F56D%400.

336. "The Fourth of July," *Daily Picayune*, July 3, 1872, afternoon edition.

337. "The Glorious Fourth," *Daily Picayune*, July 4, 1874, Saturday morning edition, sec. a.

338. "The Day We Do Not Celebrate," *Times-Picayune*, July 4, 1875.

339. Ibid.

340. "The Centennial," *Daily Picayune*, July 6, 1879.

341. Ibid.

342. "Independence Day," *Daily Picayune*, July 6, 1877.

343. BlackPast, "What, to the Slave, Is the Fourth of July?"

344. Ibid.

345. Leonard I. Sweet, "The Fourth of July and Black Americans in the Nineteenth Century: Northern Leadership Opinion within the Context of the Black Experience," *Journal of Negro History* 61, no. 3 (1976): 256–75, doi.org/10.2307/2717253.

346. Roberts, "When the Fourth of July Was a Black Holiday."

347. Ibid.

348. "Too-La-Loo for the Fourth of July," Charleston County Public Library, June 29, 2018, www.ccpl.org/charleston-time-machine/too-la-loo-fourth-july.

349. Ibid.

350. Roberts, "When the Fourth of July Was a Black Holiday."

351. Patrick Young, "When Southern Whites Boycotted and Blacks Embraced the Fourth of July During Reconstruction," *The Reconstruction Era* (blog), July 4, 2019, thereconstructionera.com/when-southern-whites-boycotted-and-blacks-embraced-the-fourth-of-july.

352. Ibid.

353. "Amidst Lightning, Thunder and Rain…," *Weekly Louisianian*, July 12, 1879.

354. "Celebrated by the Colored People," *Daily Picayune*, July 6, 1882, infoweb.newsbank.com/apps/news/document-view?p=AMNEWS&t=pubname%3A1223BCE5B718A166%21Times-Picayune&sort=YMD_date%3AA&maxresults=20&f=advanced&b=pubname&val-base-0=%22colored%22%20%22Independence%20Day%22&fld-base-0=alltext&bln-base-1=and&val-base-1=1868-1900&fld-base-1=YMD_date&fld-nav-0=YMD_date&val-nav-0=1866%20-%201900&docref=image/v2%3A1223BCE5B718A166%40EANX-1228805798840BF8%402408633-12261DEB0BFDBF78%402-124FAFBC8A618FD8%40Celebrated%2BBy%2BThe%2BColored%2BPeople.

355. W. Burlie Brown, "Louisiana and the Nation's First One-Hundredth Birthday," *Louisiana History: The Journal of the Louisiana Historical Association* 18, no. 3 (1977): 261–75, www.jstor.org/stable/4231691.

356. "Town and Country: The Centennial Celebration," *Louisiana Sugar Bowl*, July 6, 1876.

357. Ibid.

358. "Society," *Daily Picayune*, July 3, 1898, Sunday edition.

359. "One Flag Floats over One Country," *Daily Picayune*, July 5, 1898.

360. "A Great Fourth in New Orleans," *Daily Picayune*, July 5, 1901.

361. "The People's Day at the City Park," *Daily Picayune*, July 5, 1901.

362. Ibid.

363. Ibid.

364. Armstrong, *Satchmo*.

365. Ibid.

366. "Mack's Melange of Interesting Boxing, Trotting and Baseball Gossip. The Idol of the American Ring," *Times-Picayune*, July 10, 1910, infoweb.newsbank. com/apps/news/openurl?ctx_ver=z39.88-2004&rft_id=info%3Asid/infoweb. newsbank.com&svc_dat=AMNEWS&req_dat=1006417D79E1C198&rft_ val_format=info%3Aofi/fmt%3Akev%3Amtx%3Actx&rft_dat=document_ id%3Aimage%252Fv2%253A1223BCE5B718A166%2540EA NX-122B07C4660B1708%25402418863-122872DDF1145C90%254024- 12699059F9FF1DF7%2540Mack%252527s%252BMelange%252BOf%252BI nteresting%252BBoxing%25252C%252BTrotting%252Band%252BBaseball% 252BGossip.%252BThe%252BIdol%252Bof%252Bthe%252BAmerican%252 BRing/hlterms%3A%2522Mack%2527s%2520Melange%2522.

367. Jervis Anderson, "SPORT: Black Heavies," *The American Scholar* 47, no. 3 (1978): 387–95, www.jstor.org/stable/41210441.

368. Jack London, "Johnson the Victor in the Fifteenth Round," *Daily Picayune*, July 5, 1910, infoweb.newsbank.com/apps/news/document-view?p=AMNEWS&t=pu bname%3A1223BCE5B718A166%21Times-Picayune/year%3A1910%211910/ mody%3A0705%21July%2B05&b=pubname&action=browse&year=1910 &format=image&docref=image/v2%3A1223BCE5B718A166%40EANX- 122B07C12E5BF738%402418858-122872D018439FC8%400.

369. Ibid.

370. Ibid.

371. Armstrong, *Satchmo*.

372. "Two Killed and Three Wounded in Race Clash in Louisiana," *Daily Picayune*, July 5, 1910.

373. "Bloody Clashes Between Whites and Negroes. Riots in Nearly All the Large Cities in the Country," *Times-Picayune*, July 5, 1910, infoweb.newsbank.com/apps/news/ openurl?ctx_ver=z39.88-2004&rft_id=info%3Asid/infoweb.newsbank.com&svc_

dat=AMNEWS&req_dat=1006417D79E1C198&rft_val_format=info%3Aofi/
fmt%3Akev%3Amtx%3Actx&rft_dat=document_id%3Aimage%252Fv2%25
3A1223BCE5B718A166%2540EANX-122B07C12E5BF738%25402418858-
122872D018439FC8%25400-1267FCBD4A27AE16%2540Bloody%252BClash
es%252BBetween%252BWhites%252BAnd%252BNegroes.%252BRiots%252B
in%252BNearly%252BAll%252Bthe%252BLarge%252BCities%252Bin%252Bt
he/hlterms%3A%2522Jack%2520Johnson%2522.

374. "Race Riots Follow the Result of the Prize Fight. Clashes Between Whites
and Negroes Reported," *Times-Picayune*, July 6, 1910, infoweb.newsbank.com/
apps/news/openurl?ctx_ver=z39.88-2004&rft_id=info%3Asid/infoweb.
newsbank.com&svc_dat=AMNEWS&req   _dat=1006417D79E1C198&rft_
val_format=info%3Aofi/fmt%3Akev%3Amtx%3Actx&rft_dat=
document_id%3Aimage%252Fv2%253A1223BCE5B718A166%2540EA
NX-122B07C1B5293508%25402418859-122872D037D9E1D0%25402-
1265F034267994ED%2540 Race%252BRiots%252BFollow%252Bthe%252B
Result%252Bof%252Bthe%252BPrize%252BFight.%252BClashes%252BBetw
een%252BWhites%252Band%252BNegroes%252BReported/hlterms%3A%2
522Jack%2520Johnson%2522.

375. "Five Poems," *Beltway Poetry Quarterly*, www.beltwaypoetry.com/cuney/.

376. Riccardi, "Happy Birthday, Pops!"

377. Brothers, *Louis Armstrong's New Orleans*.

378. Ibid.

379. Marquis, *In Search of Buddy Bolden: First Man of Jazz*.

380. Brothers, *Louis Armstrong's New Orleans*.

381. Armstrong, *Satchmo*.

382. Riccardi, *Heart Full of Rhythm*.

383. Ricky Riccardi, "'I'm Still Louis Armstrong—Colored': Louis Armstrong
and the Civil Rights Era," That's My Home, May 11, 2020, virtualexhibits.
louisarmstronghouse.org/2020/05/11/im-still-louis-armstrong-colored-louis-
armstrong-and-the-civil-rights-era.

384. Ibid.

385. "Satchmo Tells Off, Ike, U.S.!," *Pittsburgh Courier*, September 28, 1957, www.
newspapers.com/image/40984976/?terms=Armstrong%20Blasts%20Bias%20
In%20America&match=1.

386. "How Young Reporter Got That Famous 1957 'Satchmo' Scoop," Free Online
Library.

387. Ibid.

388. "Satch Raps Segregation, Calls Off Soviet Trip," *Times-Dispatch*, September 19,
1957, www.newspapers.com/image/615873001/?terms=an%20uneducated%20
plow%20boy.&match=1.

389. "How Young Reporter Got That Famous 1957 'Satchmo' Scoop."

390. "Satch Raps Segregation, Calls Off Soviet Trip."

391. Ibid.

392. Ibid.

393. Ibid.

394. "Satchmo Sounds Off About Dixie Race Treatment," *Daily Herald*, September 1957, www.newspapers.com/image/742398209/?terms=an%20uneducated%20plow%20boy.&match=1.

395. Ibid.

396. "Satchmo Tells Off, Ike, U.S.!"

397. Ibid.

398. "On Why Jazz Isn't Cool Anymore," *Nicholas Payton* (blog), November 27, 2011, nicholaspayton.wordpress.com/2011/11/27/on-why-jazz-isnt-cool-anymore.

399. "Armstrong Party July 4 Is Canceled," *Times-Picayune States-Item*, July 1, 1986, St. Tamman edition, sec. B, infoweb.newsbank.com/apps/news/document-view?p=AMNEWS&t=pubname%3A1223BCE5B718A166%21Times-Picayune&sort=YMD_date%3AA&fld-base-0=alltext&maxresults=20&val-base-0=%22Louis%20Armstrong%27s%20birthday%22&docref=image/v2%3A1223BCE5B718A166%40EANX-1338543568B677D2%402446613-1334B18B55AB62F2%4052-1334B18B55AB62F2%40.

400. Dan Carey and Reed Branson, "Weather Can't Stop the Party," *Times-Picayune*, July 5, 1987, sec. B.

401. Andrew Smith, "Worshipers of Jazz Salute Armstrong with a Day of Music," *Times-Picayune*, July 5, 1988, sec. B.

402. Keith Spera, "Top Stories: Music," *Times-Picayune*, December 29, 2000, sec. Arts & Entertainment Weekly.

403. "Louis Armstrong New Orleans International Airport," Louis Armstrong New Orleans Airport, flymsy.com/passengers/history/.

404. Bruce Eggler, "State Unveils Satchmo Summerfest," *Times-Picayune*, March 9, 2001, sec. B.

405. Jan Ramsey, "20 Years of Satchmo SummerFest: How It All Began," *OffBeat Magazine*, www.offbeat.com/articles/20-years-satchmo-summerfest.

406. Ibid.

407. Geraldine Wyckoff, "Louis Armstrong: Born on the Fourth of July?," *OffBeat Magazine*, August 1, 2013, www.offbeat.com/articles/louis-armstrong-born-on-the-fourth-of-july.

408. Ibid.

409. Offbeat Staff, "What Does Louis Armstrong Mean?," *OffBeat Magazine*, www.offbeat.com/articles/what-does-louis-armstrong-mean/.

410. Sam Irwin, interview with Gregg Stafford, January 18, 2022.

Chapter 4

411. "Fate Marable—Pittsburgh Music History," sites.google.com/site/pittsburghmusichistory/pittsburgh-music-story/jazz/jazz---early-years/fate-marable.

412. William Howland Kenney, *Jazz on the River* (Chicago: University of Chicago Press, 2005), archive.org/details/jazzonriver0000kenn.

413. Nat Shapiro and Nat Hentoff, *Hear Me Talkin' to Ya: The Story of Jazz as Told by the Men Who Made It* (New York: Dover Publications, Inc., 1966).

414. "Steamer *Capitol* Has Wonderful Dance Orchestra," *State Times Advocate*, September 29, 1920, infoweb.newsbank.com/resources/doc/nb/image/v2%3A138FFE8785E79426%40EANX-13AE0503534B77BC%402422597-13ACB2E7519E6F42%402-13ACB2E7519E6F42%40?p=EANX.

415. "Jazz," Encyclopedia Dubuque, www.encyclopediadubuque.org/index.php?title=JAZZ.

416. Kenney, *Jazz on the River*.

417. "Joe Darensbourg interviewed by Barry Martyn."

418. Ibid.

419. Ibid.

420. Ibid.

421. Darensbourg and Vacher, *Jazz Odyssey*.

Chapter 5

422. "Jazz Standards Songs and Instrumentals (Basin Street Blues)," www.jazzstandards.com/compositions-1/basinstreetblues.htm.

423. Whitburn, *Joel Whitburn's Pop Memories, 1890–1954*.

424. Ibid.

425. "Black Requests $150,000 for New Garbage System," *Times-Picayune*, May 4, 1921.

426. Joe Gray Taylor, "New Orleans and Reconstruction," *Louisiana History: The Journal of the Louisiana Historical Association* 9, no. 3 (1968): 189–208, www.jstor.org/stable/4231016.

427. Al Rose, *Storyville, New Orleans: Being an Authentic, Illustrated Account of the Notorious Red-Light District* (Tuscaloosa: University of Alabama Press, 1974).

428. "Storyville Blaze," *Times-Picayune*, November 10, 1898.

429. Eric Criss, "Unplugging the Machine: Martin Behrman, the New Orleans Navy Yard, and the Louisiana Elections of 1920," *Louisiana History: The Journal of the Louisiana Historical Association* 61, no. 2 (2020): 133–61, www.jstor.org/stable/26921944.

430. Ibid.

431. Bill Edwards, "Spencer Walter Williams, Jr.," RagPiano.com, ragpiano.com/comps/swilliams.shtml.
432. Ibid.
433. Gary Giddins, *Visions of Jazz* (Oxford, UK: Oxford University Press, 1998).
434. Whitburn, *Joel Whitburn's Pop Memories, 1890–1954.*
435. Albert McCarthy, *Big Band Jazz* (New York: Exeter, 1983).
436. "1925–1930: The Charleston Chasers | Songs, Reviews, Credits," AllMusic, www.allmusic.com/album/1925-1930-mw0000244985.
437. Scott Yanow, "The Charleston Chasers Biography, Songs, & Albums," AllMusic, www.allmusic.com/artist/the-charleston-chasers-mn0000763109/biography.
438. Shapiro and Hentoff, *Hear Me Talkin' to Ya.*
439. "Jack Teagarden Discusses Jazz," *Times-Picayune*, September 24, 1943.
440. Ibid.
441. Cleveland Sessums, "Judy Garland Is Excited by First Glimpse of City," *Times-Picayune*, January 24, 1938.
442. Ibid.
443. Ibid.
444. Ibid.
445. "Black Requests $150,000 for New Garbage System."
446. "Andrew J. M'Shane, Lifelong Enemy of City Ring, Endorsed by O.D.A. for Orleans May," *Times-Picayune*, July 17, 1920.
447. Herman H. Diers, "Empties Basin Street," *Metronome*, August 1944.
448. Rose, *Storyville.*
449. Ibid.
450. Richard Campanella, "Today's Lafitte Greenway Was Spanish New Orleans' Carondelet Canal," *Times-Picayune*, November 17, 2017.
451. Rose, *Storyville.*
452. Ibid.
453. Richard Campanella, "Vice Districts in Antebellum New Orleans, Part II: Gallatin Street," n.d., 2.
454. Rose, *Storyville.*
455. Ibid.
456. Campanella, "Vice Districts in Antebellum New Orleans, Part II: Gallatin Street."
457. Ibid.
458. "City Intelligence—Beating a Woman," *Times-Picayune*, October 19, 1854.
459. "City Intelligence—Stabbing," *Times-Picayune*, November 8, 1854.
460. "City Intelligence—Robbery," *Times-Picayune*, January 25, 1855.
461. "City Intelligence—Attempted Assassination," *Times-Picayune*, February 1, 1855.
462. Rose, *Storyville.*

463. "Police Matters," *Times-Picayune*, September 3, 1858.

464. "The City—More Murdering," *Times-Picayune*, November 28, 1865.

465. Campanella, "Vice Districts in Antebellum New Orleans, Part II: Gallatin Street."

466. Ibid.

467. Ibid.

468. Ibid.

469. Rose, *Storyville*.

470. Campanella, "Vice Districts in Antebellum New Orleans, Part II: Gallatin Street."

471. "Local Intelligence," *New Orleans Times*, February 7, 1869.

472. "Louisiana Senator Killed by New Orleans Prostitute," HuffPost, July 16, 2007, www.huffpost.com/entry/louisiana-senator-killed-_b_56313.

473. "Local Intelligence."

474. Ibid.

475. Rose, *Storyville*.

476. "Death of Senator Beares," *Daily Picayune*, May 31, 1870.

477. Rose, *Storyville*.

478. "Carved to Death," *Daily Picayune*, November 4, 1883.

479. Rose, *Storyville*.

480. Richard Campanella, "Missed Opportunities: History's Stinging Lesson on Economic Diversification in New Orleans," NOLA.com, www.nola.com/news/business/article_8797759e-f70a-11ec-a546-832ac108619c.html.

481. Rose, *Storyville*.

482. Ibid.

483. Tiffany Renee Nelson, "Sleeping with Storyville: The Influence of Media, Race, and Morality in New Orleans' Red Light District," n.d., 102.

484. Leslie Fishbein, "Harlot or Heroine? Changing Views of Prostitution, 1870–1920," *Historian* 43, no. 1 (1980): 23–35, doi.org/10.1111/j.1540-6563.1980.tb00084.x.

485. Ibid.

486. Rose, *Storyville*.

487. Ibid.

488. Ibid.

489. Ibid.

490. Ibid.

491. "Storyville Blaze."

492. "Storyville Injunction Makes the Law Officers Hesitate about Enforcing the Law," *Times-Picayune*, July 22, 1898.

493. "Saw Storyville," *Times-Picayune*, March 13, 1899.

494. Ibid.

495. Mary A. Karnath, *Louisiana's Red-Light Districts* (Lafayette: University of Louisiana at Lafayette, n.d.).

496. Rose, *Storyville*.

497. Ibid.

498. Craig L. Foster, "Tarnished Angels: Prostitution in Storyville, New Orleans, 1900–1910," *Louisiana History: The Journal of the Louisiana Historical Association* 31, no. 4 (1990): 387–97, www.jstor.org/stable/4232839.

499. Ibid.

500. Ibid.

501. Ibid.

502. Ibid.

503. Diers, "Empties Basin Street."

504. Rose, *Storyville*.

505. Foster, "Tarnished Angels."

506. Rose, *Storyville*.

507. Armstrong, *Satchmo*.

508. Alan Lomax, *Mister Jelly Roll: The Fortunes of Jelly Roll Morton, New Orleans Creole and "Inventor of Jazz"* (Berkeley: University of California Press, 2001).

509. Ibid.

510. Rose, *Storyville*.

511. Ibid.

512. Lomax, *Mister Jelly Roll*.

513. Charles E. Kinzer, "The Tio Family: Four Generations of New Orleans Musicians, 1814–1933," vols. I and II (LSU Historical Dissertations and Theses.5522, LSU, 1993), digitalcommons.lsu.edu/gradschool_disstheses/5522. Vols. I and II.

514. Foster and as told to Tom Stoppard, *Pops Foster*.

515. Ibid.

516. Ibid.

517. Kinzer, "Tio Family."

518. Foster and as told to Tom Stoppard, *Pops Foster*.

519. Armstrong, *Satchmo*.

520. Foster and as told to Tom Stoppard, *Pops Foster*.

521. Ibid.

522. Ibid.

523. Brothers, *Louis Armstrong's New Orleans*.

524. Ibid.

525. Armstrong, *Satchmo*.

526. Ibid.

527. Foster and as told to Tom Stoppard, *Pops Foster*.

528. Lomax, *Mister Jelly Roll*.

529. Ibid.

530. Brothers, *Louis Armstrong's New Orleans*.

531. Alan Lomax, *Transcript of the 1938 Library of Congress Recordings of Jelly Roll Morton* (Coolidge Auditorium: Library of Congress, 1938).

532. Kinzer, "Tio Family."

533. Brothers, *Louis Armstrong's New Orleans*.

534. Kinzer, "Tio Family."

535. Rose, *Storyville*.

536. Kinzer, "Tio Family."

537. "Dance Hall Feud Ends in Death of Two Rivals," *Daily Picayune*, March 25, 1913, infoweb.newsbank.com/apps/news/document-view?p=AM NEWS&t=pubname%3A1223BCE5B718A166%21Times-Picayune/ year%3A1913%211913/mody%3A0325%21March%2B25&action=brows e&format=image&docref=image/v2%3A1223BCE5B718A166%40EANX-122ABF08EB7D7028%402419852-122877E6AAEE3430%400.

538. Ibid.

539. Ibid.

540. Kinzer, "Tio Family."

541. Ibid.

542. Rose, *Storyville*.

543. Ibid.

544. "Dance Hall Feud Ends in Death of Two Rivals."

545. Rose, *Storyville*.

546. Karl Koenig, "Tango Belt," Jazz music, BasinStreet.com, 1996, basinstreet. com/wp-content/uploads/2016/09/43-tangobelt.pdf.

547. "Dance Hall Feud Ends in Death of Two Rivals."

548. Ibid.

549. Ibid.

550. Ibid.

551. Ibid.

552. Ibid.

553. Rose, *Storyville*.

554. Rose.

555. "Dance Hall Feud Ends in Death of Two Rivals."

556. Koenig, "Tango Belt."

557. Kinzer, "Tio Family."

558. Ibid.

559. Ibid.

560. Rose, *Storyville*.

561. "Jass and Jassism," *Times-Picayune*, June 20, 1918.

562. "The Jazz and the Public Dance," *Louisiana Weekly*, March 6, 1926.

563. "State Music Teachers Denounce Jazz Music," *Daily Signal*, March 19, 1921.

564. Charles Suhor, *Jazz in New Orleans: The Postwar Years Through 1970* (Lanham, MD: Scarecrow Press, 2001).

565. E. Belfield Spriggins, "Excavating Local Jazz," *Louisiana Weekly*, April 23, 1933.

566. J. Mark Souther, "Making the 'Birthplace of Jazz': Tourism and Musical Heritage Marketing in New Orleans," *Louisiana History: The Journal of the Louisiana Historical Association* 44, no. 1 (2003): 39–73, www.jstor.org/stable/4233901.

567. Ibid.

568. Ibid.

569. Sterling A. Brown, "Farewell to Basin Street," *Record Changer*, December 1944.

570. Ibid.

571. Brown, "Farewell to Basin Street."

572. Souther, "Making the 'Birthplace of Jazz.'"

573. Lawrence W. Levine, "Jazz and American Culture," *Journal of American Folklore* 102, no. 403 (1989): 6–22, doi.org/10.2307/540078.

574. Ibid.

575. Ibid.

576. Paul Mallon and United Press, "La Follette Denounces Ku Klux Klan Openly Today," *Imperial Valley Press*, August 8, 1924.

577. Levine, "Jazz and American Culture."

578. Ibid.

579. Suhor, *Jazz in New Orleans*.

580. Ibid.

581. Danton Walker, "Broadway," *Daily News*, September 22, 1944.

582. Riccardi, *Heart Full of Rhythm*.

583. "Amusements Calendar," *Times-Picayune*, January 12, 1945.

584. Louis Armstrong, "Reel-to-Reel Tape Recorded by Louis Armstrong—Louis Tape 24—Track 4" (New Orleans, 1945), collections.louisarmstronghouse.org/asset-detail/1111280.

585. Ibid.

586. Ibid.

587. "New Incinerator Planned by City," *Times-Picayune*, January 23, 1945.

588. John Lewis Stone, "Basin Street to Be Rededicated [*sic*] in New Orleans," *Advocate*, January 16, 1945.

589. Suhor, *Jazz in New Orleans*.

590. Rose, *Storyville*.

591. Lind, "Song Satirist Benny Grunch Thinks His New Orleans Nostalgia Is More Relevant Now Than Ever."

592. Suhor, *Jazz in New Orleans*.

593. Souther, "Making the 'Birthplace of Jazz.'"

594. Suhor, *Jazz in New Orleans*.

595. Ibid.

596. Ibid.

597. Ibid.

598. "News Views," *Princeton Daily Clarion*, January 23, 1945, www.newspapers.com/image/437618752/?terms=%22Basin%20Street%20back%22&match=1.

599. Edwards, "Spencer Walter Williams, Jr."

600. Ibid.

601. Ibid.

Chapter 6

602. Shapiro and Hentoff, *Hear Me Talkin' to Ya*.

603. Ibid.

604. Austin Sonnier Jr., *Willie Geary "Bunk" Johnson: The New Iberia Years* (New York: Crescendo Publishing, 1977).

605. "Joe Darensbourg interviewed by Barry Martyn."

606. Sonnier, *Second Linin'*.

607. Hazeldine and Martyn, *Bunk Johnson: Song of the Wanderer*.

608. Hal Smith, "Bunk Johnson," San Francisco Traditional Jazz Foundation Collection—Spotlight at Stanford, June 2, 2018, exhibits.stanford.edu/sftjf/feature/bunk-johnson.

609. Hazeldine and Martyn, *Bunk Johnson: Song of the Wanderer*.

610. Smith, "Bunk Johnson."

611. "Labor Day Fittingly Celebrated," *State Times*, September 3, 1917.

612. "Joe Darensbourg Interviewed by Barry Martyn."

613. Darensbourg and Vacher, *Jazz Odyssey*.

614 *Baton Rouge City Directory*, 1922.

615. "Joe Darensbourg Interviewed by Barry Martyn."

616. Darensbourg and Vacher, *Jazz Odyssey*.

617. Ibid.

618. "Joe Darensbourg Interviewed by Barry Martyn."

619. Darensbourg and Vacher, *Jazz Odyssey*.

620. Ibid.

621. Ibid.

622. Eddie "Big Head" Johnson, "Music Rising—The Musical Cultures of the Gulf South," musicrising.tulane.edu/discover/people/eddie-big-head-johnson.

623. Ibid.

624. "Israel Gorman," Music Rising—The Musical Cultures of the Gulf South," musicrising.tulane.edu/discover/people/israel-gorman/.

625. Eddie "Big Head" Johnson, November 6, 1962, musicrising.tulane.edu/listen/interviews/eddie-big-head-johnson-1962-11-06/.

626. "Joe Darensbourg Interviewed by Barry Martyn."

627. Darensbourg and Vacher, *Jazz Odyssey*.

628. Paige Vanvorst, "Joe Darensbourg," *Jazzbeat*, May 25, 2005.

629. Darensbourg and Vacher, *Jazz Odyssey*.

630. Ibid.

631. Ernest H. Miller, *Baton Rouge City Directory*, vol. VI, Delata (Asheville, NC: Piedmont Directory Co., 1913).

632. Darensbourg and Vacher, *Jazz Odyssey*.

633. Ibid.

634. Ibid.

635. Ibid.

636. Al Rose and Edmond Souchon, *New Orleans Jazz: A Family Album* (Louisiana State University Press, 1967).

637. Darensbourg and Vacher, *Jazz Odyssey*.

638. Ibid.

639. Ibid.

640. Ibid.

641. "Joe Darensbourg Interviewed by Barry Martyn."

642. Ibid.

643. Karl Koenig, "Trinity of Early Jazz Leaders; John Robichaux, 'Toots' Johnson, Claiborne Williams," Jazz music, BasinStreet.Com, basinstreet.com/wp-content/uploads/2016/09/trinity.pdf.

644. "Contest Now On for King of Baton Rouge," *New Advocate*, February 8, 1912.

645. "Want a King What Has Got Some Quality," *New Advocate*, February 13, 1912.

646. "Just Look What Has Happened to King Joe, First," *New Advocate*, February 20, 1912.

647. Ibid.

648. "Two Kings Certain for Mardi Gras," *New Advocate*, January 30, 1913.

649. "Toots Is King of Carnival for Few Hours," *State*, February 25, 1914.

650. "No More Mardi Gras Parades in Baton Rouge," *State Times*, March 2, 1914, infoweb.newsbank.com/apps/news/document-view?p=AMNEWS&t=pubname%3A138FFE8785E79426%21State%2BTimes%2BAdvocate&sort=YMD_date%3AA&fld-base-0=alltext&maxresults=20&val-base-0=%22Toots%20Johnson%22%20%22parade%22&b=pubname&docref=image/v2%3A138FFE8785E79426%40EANX-13A86013936FD236%402420194-13A7BA308B3CB532%407-13A7BA308B3CB532%40.

651. Ibid.

652. Ibid.

653. Ibid.

654. Matthew Albridge and Charles Lussier, "Baton Rouge Has Mardi Gras Parades, but Why Doesn't It Have Any on Fat Tuesday?," The *Advocate*, March 4, 2022, www.theadvocate.com/baton_rouge/news/article_d76f69aa-9986-11ec-b5dc-9bb5f8654fe7.html.

655. "Cancelling Carnival: The Times That Mardi Gras Was Called Off," Where Y'at New Orleans, www.whereyat.com/cancelling-carnival-the-times-that-mardi-gras-was-called-off.

656. Foster and as told to Tom Stoppard, *Pops Foster*.

657. Ibid.

658. "Hears Music of Toots Johnson's Band above Broadway," *State Times*, June 26, 1923.

659. "Weather Vane, The," *Buffalo Evening News*, June 18, 1923.

660. Ibid.

661. "Toot Johnson, Colored Band Leader, Is Dead," *Daily Signal*, March 27, 1928, http://acadia.advantage-preservation.com.

662. Associated Press, "Orchestra Leader Dead," *Shreveport Journal*, March 27, 1928.

663. Associated Press, "Negro Jazz King Makes Final March," *Wichita Falls Record News*, March 28, 1928.

664. Associated Negro Press, "Unique Orchestra Leader Succumbs," *Pittsburgh Courier*, April 7, 1928.

Chapter 7

665. Foster and as told to Tom Stoppard, *Pops Foster*.

666. Darensbourg and Vacher, *Jazz Odyssey*.

667. John Chapman, "First Jazz Men," *Daily News*, January 3, 1937.

668. H.O. (Harry O.) Brunn, *The Story of the Original Dixieland Jazz Band* (New York: Da Capo Press, 1977), archive.org/details/storyoforiginald0000brun.

669. Al Rose and Edmond Souchon, *New Orleans Jazz: A Family Album*, Revised Edition (Baton Rouge: Louisiana State University Press, 1967).

670. Brunn, *Story of the Original Dixieland Jazz Band*.

671. Darensbourg and Vacher, *Jazz Odyssey*.

672. "Bursts and Duds," *American Legion Weekly*, December 12, 1924.

673. Foster and as told to Tom Stoppard, *Pops Foster*.

674. Holly Hobbs, "Papa John Joseph," 64 Parishes, 64parishes.org/entry/papa-john-joseph.

675. Ibid.

676. Ibid.

677. "'Papa John,' 90, Marches In Just After Saints," *Sunday Advocate*, January 24, 1965, sec. B.

ABOUT THE AUTHOR

The day after New Orleans musician Allen Toussaint died in 2015, author Sam Irwin listened to trumpeter Nicholas Payton's brilliant performance on Toussaint's *The Bright Mississippi*. Inspired, he picked up his horn after a thirty-year layoff and started practicing. He hasn't stopped yet and is now the trumpet bandleader of the Florida Street Blowhards, a Baton Rouge–based traditional jazz band.

A public relations professional and freelance journalist, Irwin has been writing about Louisiana for the last two decades. He is the public relations director of the American Sugar Cane League and former press secretary of the Louisiana Department of Agriculture and Forestry.

He grew up in Breaux Bridge, Louisiana, the Crawfish Capital of the World, and wrote about that experience in *Louisiana Crawfish: A Succulent History of the Cajun Crustacean* in 2014. He followed that book up with *It Happens in Louisiana: Peculiar Tales, Traditions and Recipes from the Bayou* in 2015.

The former music major at the University of Louisiana at Lafayette is spending more time playing trumpet with the FSB at front-yard concerts, wedding second lines and other gigs than writing. He lives in an old neighborhood in Baton Rouge with his wife, two cornets, two trumpets and a Benge fluegelhorn. Another horn can be expected at any time.

Visit us at
www.historypress.com